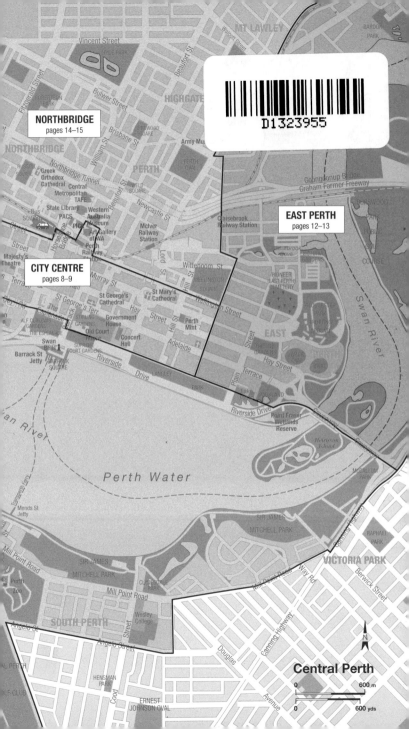

INSIGHT GUIDES

PERTH

smart guide

Contents

Below: a team from the Surf Life Saving Club hits the water.

Below: enjoying the city skyline from Kings Park.

Perth

It is Australia's most isolated state capital, on the world's most isolated continent. It is no wonder, then, that Perth has a strong sense of cheerful indifference towards the activities of the rest of Australia. Perth prides itself on the sparkling waters off the coast, its laid-back locals and a lifestyle that is centred around getting out into the natural beauties that surround the city.

Perth Facts and Figures

Population: 2.3 million in Western Australia,
1.7 million in Perth greater metropolitan area
Indigenous population: 3.4 percent
Population born overseas: 42 percent
Area: 5,386 sq km (2,080 sq miles)
Population density: 310 people per sq km
(817 per sq mile)
Language: English, but around 25 percent speak another language at home
Distance from London: 14,000km (8,700 miles), with an approximate flying time of 17 hours and 30 minutes
Locals' top activity: 'eating out at a restaurant'
Nickname: 'sandgropers', for an unusual insect found in WA

The Most Remote Capital

Perth is a paradox: a state capital city that still feels like a holiday town. Isolated by the bush, ocean, desert and rolling agricultural land, it remains the most remote state capital in the world. Its special appeal as a city lies in the fact that it is a place where a big-city sophistication combines with small-town friendliness. And of course, it has some spectacular natural splendours on its doorstep, with kilometres of golden beaches and good proximity to the rolling green lands of the Swan Valley. Perth is located on the west coast of Western Australia, the country's largest state, which brings in the majority of the nation's GDP thanks to its wealth of natural resources, in spite of much of the state being uninhabited and home only to scrubby bush.

Captain James Stirling founded the City of Perth as part of the Swan River colony in 1829. Although the territory was claimed by Britain, explorers from countries such as Holland and France had been visiting WA since the early 1600s, and the land had been the home of indigenous people for around 50,000 years. The colony officially lasted until 1832, and Perth trundled along until the 1890s, when the discovery of gold turned it into a city. Riches from the Kalgoorlie goldfields paid for hundreds of public buildings as the government of the day struggled to cope with the tide of newcomers.

Looking to the Future

Perth today is an affluent, prosperous city. Though the goldfields have been exploited, the nickel, iron and gas resources found in Western Australia are fuelling another boom and new expansion, drawing skilled migrants from around the world and regenerating the inner city with tourism-driven ventures, new homes and commercial towers. With the influx of new residents and the cultures they bring, Perth is becoming ever more cosmopolitan. Currently, billions of state government dollars are being poured into the Perth City Link project. Due for completion by 2017, this is a dynamic venture

Below: outside Council House, bronze sculptures of a recognisable Australian icon.

that is joining the CBD's far west end to North-bridge's cultural centre via a network of tree-lined boulevards, modern inner-city apartment buildings and leafy public spaces. Add an influx of trendy bars and cafés (made possible by the recent relaxing of liquor licensing laws) and the Perth city centre is becoming an increasingly vibrant place to be and be seen. Plans for a major redevelopment of the Swan River frontage, on which the city of Perth is perched, also kick off later in 2012.

The People of Perth

Local people enjoy a fairly relaxed lifestyle. With excellent year-round weather, there is a strong emphasis on the outdoors. Enjoying free time at weekends often centres around taking advantage of getting outside, whether that's taking the dog to the beach, the kids to a local park or catching up with friends over a Sunday afternoon beer at a favourite pub. While having a good time is high on everyone's list, local people are keen to be a part of the state's prosperity, and working hard before hitting the beach is the norm. Meanwhile, many workers have been taking advantage of the current minerals boom in the north of the state and moving out. This is causing frequent staff shortages, especially as tourist numbers rise. Visitors are increasingly discovering the sunny charms of this laid-back city that knows how to enjoy the good life it has made for itself.

Highlights

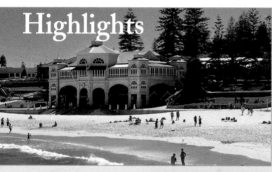

▲ **Cottesloe Beach** Great for swimming, lazing on golden sands and watching glorious sunsets over the Indian Ocean.
▶ **City views from Kings Park** Get a bird's-eye view of the city and the sprawling Swan River.

▲ **Rottnest Island** A 45-minute ferry ride from the Perth CBD lie turquoise swimming bays and a cool holiday vibe.

▶ **Café culture in Fremantle** Spend some time watching the world go by on Fremantle's 'cappuccino strip'.

▲ **Swan Valley wineries** Sample world-class wines at the Swan Valley's cellar doors.
▶ **Aussie Rules football** Head to an Eagles or Dockers game along with sports-mad locals throughout winter.

Swan River
and Kings Park

The Swan River and Kings Park are synonymous with Perth. The Swan River curls around the edge of the Central Business District (CBD) and extends its arms through suburbs, heading south to Fremantle and east to the Swan Valley. The river is an integral part of the city's culture, giving locals a place to walk, cycle, boat, play and fish. Kings Park is perched above the Swan River and overlooks the CBD, offering an inner-city retreat filled with walkways, spectacular views and rare flora.

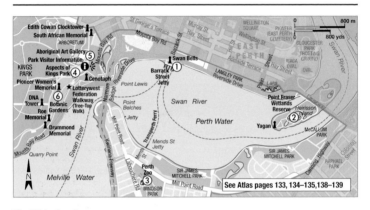

The Waterfront

The waterfront south of the city centre focuses on **Barrack Street Jetty** and the **Swan Bells** ①. Immense copper sails cup a green-glass bell tower *(see box, right)*. The bells, a gift from the church of St Martin-in-the-Fields in London, were installed here to mark Australia's bicentenary in 1988. They rang in the New Year in London for 275 years and have proclaimed the coronation of every British monarch from George II in 1727. There's a small charge to see the bells and take the lift to the outside observation level, which has great views.

The jetty is the departure point for river cruises to Fremantle and up to the wineries in the Swan Valley, as well as the ferry to South Perth. There are a few coffee and food options on the jetty, ranging from 'pay what you can afford' Hare Krishna cuisine at Annalakshmi, to fine dining on the waterfront at **Halo**. If you are patient, you may even see some dolphins flit past.

Walking up Barrack Street will take you to St George's Terrace. This is the heart of the business area *(see p.8)*, where folk in suits rush around trying not to get blown over by the winds that can funnel down the terrace. Modern office towers rub elbows with colonial buildings, and the two are easy to confuse.

SEE ALSO RESTAURANTS, P.100; TRANSPORT, P.121

Heirisson Island

The walk from Barrack Street Jetty to **Heirisson Island** ②, which is bisected by the Causeway, can be done comfortably in half an hour. A small colony of Western Grey kangaroos are housed in an enclosure here; move quietly around the track and you may be able to spot them grazing. At the southern tip of the island there is a bronze statue of Yagan, an Aboriginal leader killed in 1833.

Named for a French sailor, François Heirisson, who rowed a longboat upriver to the island from his moored ship *Le Naturaliste*, Heirisson

Left: the Swan Bells.

Kings Park

No other city in the world has such a large area of natural bushland at its heart. The cultivated gardens with lawns, terraces and water gardens are substantial, but form only a small part of the 400-hectare (988-acre) site, which is mainly native bush. Free guided walks conducted by volunteer guides leave daily from September to June at 10am, 12pm and 2pm from **Aspects of Kings Park** ④. The park is full of memorials, for example, commemorating those lost in two world wars, the Boer War and the Bali bombing of 2002.

Along Fraser Avenue there is a choice of eateries with river views, like Frasers Restaurant, given a complete face-lift in 2011 for the Commonwealth Heads of Government meeting. On the river side of Fraser Avenue, opposite the restaurant, the **Aboriginal Art Gallery** ⑤ sells fine indigenous arts and crafts. It usually has an Aboriginal artist in residence.

Beyond the Cenotaph at the end of Fraser Avenue is the heavily planted **Botanic Gardens** ⑥. By keeping to the path, with the Swan on your left, you will come to a spectacular Tree-Top Walk with views across the river.

SEE ALSO ABORIGINAL CULTURE, P.27; PARKS, P.89–91

Island has been a site of political controversy. In 1984, an Aboriginal camp lasted for 40 days before its occupants, land-rights protesters, were evicted. In 2012 fresh protests saw land-rights activists camp on the island for over six weeks.
SEE ALSO PARKS, P.88–9

The South Bank

Over the Causeway, riverside parkland leads back

Below: walking in Kings Park.

downriver, with a café, boat ramp and boat hire at Coode Street in South Perth. At Mends Street, the Transperth ferry departs for Barrack Street every half-hour during the day, every 15 minutes at peak commuting times. Mends Street has several eating options, and the **Perth Zoo** ③ is a short stroll from this junction, along Labouchere Road.

When the zoo opened in 1897, six keepers looked after two lions and a tiger. Now there are around 190 different species totalling more than 1,100 animals. One of the highlights is the Australian Bushwalk through re-creations of different Australian ecosystems, including a tropical rainforest. There are no fences in this section, so you can get up close with kangaroos and other native fauna.
SEE ALSO CHILDREN, P.38; TRANSPORT, P.121

When visiting the Swan Bell Tower, take note of the impressive copper sails which enclose the glass tower. In the 1980s 1- and 2-cent copper coins, rendered virtually useless by inflation, were phased out of circulation. These coins have been melted down and used in the bell tower's sails.

City Centre

Perth's city centre is made up of a short stretch of skyscrapers and office blocks, with older buildings and shopping to the north of St George's Terrace. Economic boom times have seen office space in Perth stretch to its absolute limit, making it the tightest market in Australia. With the Swan River on one side of the city and Kings Park bordering another, it is a small, concentrated area of commerce and retail, kept buoyant by the state's prosperous resources industry. The recent liberalisation of liquor licensing laws has seen small themed bars pop up all over the CBD. Visitors and locals alike have feverishly embraced this inner-city rejuvenation.

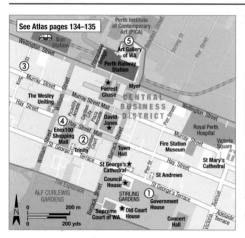

See Atlas pages 134–135

Perth is a city on the move. Construction has started on the Perth City Link project, which will seamlessly link Northbridge and the city, as currently there is no pleasant way to walk between the two areas. The CBD foreshore is also staring down the barrel of a large Sydney Harbour-style redevelopment, as is the link between the city and South Perth. Depending when you visit, you will notice varying degrees of construction.

The CBD

The Central Business District converges upon the grid of streets north of Barrack Street Jetty. St George's Terrace, Hay Street and Murray Street run east–west, with King Street, William Street and Barrack Street running north–south. Most offices are located on St George's Terrace, with the bulk of retail happening on Hay, Murray and King streets.

Historic Perth

When Perth city centre was redeveloped, many historical buildings were demolished. However, the best place to see those that survived is **St George's Terrace**, Perth's first thoroughfare, stretching the length of the CBD and centring on **Stirling Gardens**, where a collection of buildings date back to the founding of Perth.

Along the terrace you'll see the **Old Court House**, built in 1836, next door to **Government House** ①, the residence of the state governor, to the rear of Stirling Gardens. The Old Court House shares the gardens with the Supreme Court of WA (1903). It was here that the first settlers pitched their tents in 1829. Alongside the gardens is **Council House**,

Left: the towers of the CBD.

Left: shoppers in the Murray Street Mall.

You'll also find plenty of shops, including the Myer department complex, in Forrest Chase, a central area between Wellington Street and the **Murray Street Mall**.
SEE ALSO SHOPPING, P.109

Cultural Perth

The Perth Cultural Centre lies north of the railway tracks, joining the CBD with Northbridge; it is most easily accessed via the walkway over Wellington Street from Forrest Chase shopping mall. On the city centre side, the **Art Gallery of Western Australia** ⑤ is the main building to the right after you cross into the centre, its slab-sided face generally advertising its latest exhibition. Inside, several floors of modern, well-lit galleries display more than 1,000 Australian and international works of art. Significant Australian artists include Arthur Streeton, Frederick McCubbin and Brett Whitely. There is also a large Aboriginal art gallery and regular, free public tours.
SEE ALSO MUSEUMS AND GALLERIES, P.76–7

the modern headquarters of Perth City Council. Nearby **St George's Cathedral** was begun in 1879 and completed in 1888, four years before the Western Australia gold rush. An extensive restoration programme was completed in 2008.

West along St Georges Terrace is **London Court** ②, one of only a few major building projects dating from the 1930s depression. The mock-Tudor ambience is enhanced by a narrow alley, bijou shops and decorative porticoes at each end, one in Hay Street Mall, the other on St George's Terrace, the latter topped by a St George and the Dragon clock. Of all the city centre's arcades, this is the one to comb for Australiana (koala badges, emu-leather handbags, kangaroo-fur coin purses), jewellery and other gifts.
SEE ALSO PARKS, P.91; SHOPPING, P.109

The Shopping Centre

King Street ③, on the west end of the grid, was once dubbed 'the Paris end of Perth'. While no doubt this was originally just a nice bit of marketing, the name has stuck. While you have to squint to see Paris in King Street, it is undoubtedly the stylish end of town. Big-name luxury brands make themselves at home next to über-cool clothing and shoe shops, as well as several cafés.

A warren of shopping malls and arcades lies between St George's Terrace and Wellington Street, each with its own individual character. **Hay Street Mall** ④ is home to many retailers, including the **enex100** retail complexwhich opened in 2009, and national department store group **David Jones**, where you will find some of Australia's best fashion designers, a gourmet food hall and lots more.

Below: sculpture in the grounds of the Art Gallery of WA.

Leederville

Located a couple of minutes' drive from the city of Perth, Leederville is the place to come if you seek a relaxed inner-city vibe. The district has a distinctly European-influenced air, with excellent delis and other eateries packing the streets. Indeed, other than eating, the main activity in Leederville is people-watching, usually from a sidewalk table at one of the myriad cafés dotted along the Oxford Street strip. The suburb has a laid-back, urban feel – cool kids with facial piercings make themselves at home next to young families having coffee with their pet dog by their side. Hip boutiques and popular pubs round out the bohemian ambience.

The History of Leederville

The Leederville area was initially founded by private settlers William Leeder and John Monger. Between 1850 and 1868 Perth experienced rapid growth, with 10,000 convicts arriving. With the added pressure for food, Leederville's wetlands areas were primarily used as market gardens and dairy and poultry farms.

After World War II, migration policy was changed and a large number of European migrants arrived in Perth. Many of these settled in the Leederville and North Perth areas, drawn to the cheap land and large amounts of market-garden space. Today the market gardens have well and truly disappeared, and Leederville is one of the trendy suburbs of Perth, located only 4km (2.5 miles) from the city centre.

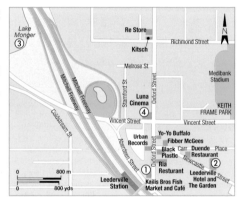

Oxford Street

Heading up Oxford Street immediately gives you a sense of what Leederville is all about. The large Continental European migrant population that settled in Leederville many years ago, well before the suburb was remotely trendy, has ensured that the culture is centred around food, relaxing with friends over a coffee and watching the world go by.

On the main part of Oxford Street you will walk past the large **Kailis Bros Fish Market** ①. The Kailis family originally came from Greece, and now their seafood business is just about the largest in WA, supplying restaurants, cafés and supermarkets. They have a large fresh seafood and café outlet in Leederville. Continuing your culinary journey along Oxford Street, you will find more cafés per square centimetre than it seems anyone could reasonably need.

Left: fresh fish at Kailis'.

Left: strolling in Leederville.

being just a sample of those on offer. There are a few interesting shops and boutiques worth a look, too, often reflecting the quirky nature of the suburb.

The main action on Oxford Street ends at the Vincent Street intersection. On one of the intersection's corners is the Art Deco-style building of the **Luna Cinema** ④. Red carpet and a big staircase set the mood; the main theatre is a grand example of the architecture and is a great place to escape the summer heat. The Luna shows films that you won't find at the big complexes, and in the summer runs an outdoor cinema next door, where punters can bring a picnic and a bottle of wine and enjoy a film from a deckchair in the warm night air.

If you continue up Oxford Street away from the central buzz, you will quickly come across the popular Italian deli, **The Re Store**. The smells of cured meats, exceptional cheese and yeasty bread hit you instantly and are only the start of things on offer here. If you can speak Italian you will be fussed over even more.

SEE ALSO FILM, P.57; FOOD AND DRINK, P.61

However, it can be surprisingly difficult to get a table on a Sunday morning, when locals flock here to read the papers and sip a latte, while competing with lycra-clad cyclists who descend on the strip with bikes in tow.

The **Leederville Hotel** and trendy bar, **The Garden** ② occupies one of Leederville's oldest buildings, dating from 1897; the architect remains unknown. Extensive alterations and additions were made in the 1920s and 1960s. On the corner of Oxford and Vincent is the old post office, built in 1897. Now a café, it still retains its original character and terracotta Marseilles-patterned tiled roof.

SEE ALSO FOOD AND DRINK, P.60–1; PUBS AND BARS, P.97; RESTAURANTS, P.102

Lake Monger

A short stroll west along Vincent Street, crossing under the freeway overpass, will take you to **Lake Monger** ③. Prior to white settlement of the area, Lake Monger was known as Galup to the land's indigenous people, the Nyungar. Galup was a site used by Aborigines for camping, hunting and fishing. Today Lake Monger is home to a large group of black swans – WA's state emblem. You can stroll around the 3.5km (2.2-mile) lake, or just take a shorter walk through the bird habitat area on purpose-built boardwalks.

The lake is surrounded by weeping willows and other lovely trees, and on one side there is a children's playground. The track around the lake is popular with walkers, joggers and cyclists.

Eating and Entertainment

Cuisines from around the world are well represented, with Spanish, French, Malay, Indonesian, Turkish, Mongolian and Vietnamese foods

Once a year Oxford Street is shut off to cars and a leg of the Perth Criterium series is held here. The best cyclists in town descend on Oxford Street and race in a series of heart-in-your-throat laps at top speeds. Sometimes there are spectacular crashes as bikes and riders go akimbo, but there is always great action as well as a fantastic vibe. It usually happens in late January or early February.

East Perth

E ast Perth is becoming a spectacular gateway to the city, a riverside precinct for living and socialising that is taking shape out of a former industrial wasteland. Its main area, Riverside, is set to develop further over the next decade, but the rebuilding of East Perth that began in the early 1990s is already a sight to see. The central Royal Street and Plain Street are where you'll find the buzzing centre of shops, cafés and restaurants. When redevelopment started in the early 1990s, state government allocated one percent of the cost of landscape and architectural projects to public art. The results are dotted along the banks of the inlet and throughout the district.

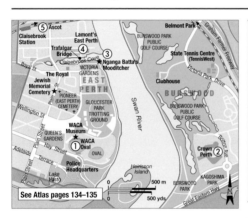

See Atlas pages 134–135

A short walk up Plain Street off Royal Street is where you'll find the colony's earliest link with its own history. Two new town houses on Plain Street have unique back gardens. Peer through their iron gates, and you'll find the Jewish Memorial Cemetery. The houses are built over the original Hebrew burial grounds that opened in 1867. About 30 people were buried here before a new cemetery opened for people of all faiths in 1899.

Arriving in East Perth

The deck of a boat on the Swan River is the place to stand and take a first look at East Perth. Cruisers from Barrack Street Jetty motor past the north bank, where the slender towers of the **Western Australian Cricket Association** (WACA) ① ground are prominent. Closer to the foreshore and its wetlands area are the heritage-listed police headquarters, and behind the WACA is **Gloucester Park** harness-racing track.

Boats sail under the Causeway, passing Heirisson Island before sighting the distinctive, pyramid-shaped **Crown Perth** ②

(formerly Burswood Entertainment Complex) on the south bank.

SEE ALSO NIGHTLIFE, P.84; SPORTS, P.113; TRANSPORT, P.121

Around Claisebrook Cove

The best of East Perth, however, is yet to come, on a northerly diversion off the Swan and into **Claisebrook Cove** ③, a stream of fresh water found by Captain Stirling in his 1827 exploration of the river. He called it Clause Creek, after the ship's surgeon, Clause, which later evolved into Claisebrook.

Leisure grounds at the mouth of the inlet give way to houses and apartments, with restaurants and cafés fringing

the waterway. A footbridge, Trafalgar Bridge, crosses Claisebrook, and footpaths and cycle paths run around it. One of Perth's best restaurants, **Lamont's East Perth** ④, looks over the water to Burswood. Cruise boats can go no further along the waterway, but you can proceed on foot. The elimination of motor traffic and the encouragement of walking and bike-riding is part of the East Perth ethos.

An interesting architectural mix is a vital element of the new East Perth. Influences range from Oriental, Regency and traditional European to concrete and steel, with a broad spectrum of materials and colours to

Left: Claisebrook Cove.

Perth's **Crown Casino** can also be found here, as part of Crown Perth, the city's premier hospitality precinct. The complex is also home to two hotels, a number of top-end restaurants, a public golf course and the permanently inflated **Dome**, which plays host to concerts and sporting events such as the annual Hopman Cup tennis tournament in January.

The casino offers all the usual gambling options, of course, such as blackjack, roulette, baccarat, pai gow, poker, Caribbean stud and craps 24 hours a day, except Christmas Day, Good Friday and Anzac Day.

SEE ALSO NIGHTLIFE, P.84; SPORTS, P.113–14, 115

match that diversity. This is inner-city living with style. Everyone has a veranda, patio or terrace, but there is no space for private gardens. This makes public parks like Victoria Gardens, with its free barbecues and picnic tables under the trees, and **Queen's Gardens**, landscaped with lily ponds and English trees, all the busier.

Like so much of Perth, Claisebrook is an ancient area with powerful Aboriginal links. This river-bank area is known as **Nganga Batta's Mooditcher** (Sunshine's Living Strength) and is a 'place of hope and friendship' for Aboriginal people. The standing stones on the foreshore form a winding trail, the **Illa Kurri Sacred Dreaming Path**, which describes the chain of lakes and wetlands spanning the land before Perth was built.

SEE ALSO RESTAURANTS, P.102–3

Racing and the Casino

Watching horse racing is very popular in Australia, and **Ascot** ⑤, with its grand 1900s buildings and grandstand, is WA's principal racecourse, used for summer racing (in winter the action moves to **Belmont Park** at Goodwood Parade, Burswood). Experts regard Ascot's 300m/yd inclining straight as the toughest test of stayers in Australia.

Below: the towers of the WACA grounds.

Cricket

There are few better places to experience the national sport in all its forms than the grounds of the WACA, WA's governing cricket body founded in 1885. More than 40 days of first-class cricket are played each summer season (Oct–Mar) ranging through international one-day matches, Test matches and inter-state contests. The WACA provides special shuttles on match days, running to the ground from the Wellington Street Bus Station in the city, via the train and additional bus stations; regular bus services to the WACA ground include Transperth's free red CAT bus.

Even if there isn't a match to watch, you may want to visit the WACA's Museum, where you can discover more about the history of the club and many of the great international cricketers.

SEE ALSO SPORTS, P.113

Northbridge

Cut off from the city centre by the Perth–Fremantle railway, Northbridge, an old and distinctive neighbourhood packed with heritage-listed buildings, has evolved separately from the CBD, even though it is just a short hop away over the Horseshoe Bridge. During the day, Northbridge is the place to come for sourcing interesting European and Asian foods at bargain prices, while at weekends it turns into Perth's night-time hot spot. Clubs, bars, pubs and restaurants heave into the wee small hours as people dance, eat and drink the weekend away. A thriving cultural life rounds out the area and ensures its place as one of Perth's most interesting districts.

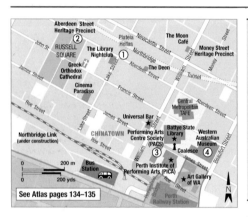

See Atlas pages 134–135

The **Perth City Link** is a redevelopment plan which will unite Northbridge with the city centre by submerging the Wellington Street bus and rail stations, linking King Street on the south with Northbridge's Lake Street in a continuous stream of galleries, cafés and entertainments. One of the most important elements of the project is a new entertainment and sports stadium. The project is due to be completed by the end of 2012.

Northbridge's Culture and Heritage

The longest-established communities of Perth, after the Aborigines and the British, are Mediterranean Europeans, who began arriving in WA after World War II. The dome of the **Greek Orthodox Cathedral** in Russell Square is a striking symbol of that time. The next significant wave of immigrants was Asian, and the little Chinatown at the east end of James and Roe streets shows its influence.

A Mediterranean atmosphere prevails in Northbridge on long summer evenings. The area is ideal for strolling in the early evening, alfresco dining, and dawdling as you watch the passing parade. The intersection of Lake and James streets, the hub of the entertainment district, is a good place to linger over a drink and take Northbridge's pulse. Almost every restaurant makes use of the pavement, and on a warm evening they're all bustling.

A more recent feature that represents the area's culture are the distinctive polished-concrete pillars, based on Classical Greek architecture, on **Plateia Hellas** ① on Lake Street. An homage to the local Greek community, this versatile space allows vehicle movement and parking as well as community activities such as performances and small festivals. The square is considered the jewel in the crown of Northbridge's redevelopment.

Meanwhile, the **Aberdeen Street Heritage Precinct** ② contains nine buildings that have been retained due to their heritage, streetscape and economic value.

SEE ALSO WALKS AND VIEWS, P.123–4

Contemporary Arts

WA's creative arts scene centres on the end of Lake Street, near the WA Art Gallery, where the CBD currently joins with Northbridge. Called the Perth Cultural Centre, it is where the arts, culture, archives and community activity come together.

Left: enjoying a few beers at the Brass Monkey pub.

paintings. The oldest life fossil known is displayed here; it was discovered in 1999 in the Pilbara region. The museum has a pleasant coffee shop next to the **Old Gaol**, built by convicts in 1855–6 and now crammed with memorabilia of Perth life since James Stirling's expedition of 1829, including a complete original courtroom, a pedal radio that kept outback families in touch, and a complete pharmacy from 1917.

SEE ALSO CHILDREN, P.38–9; MUSEUMS AND GALLERIES, P.77–8

A Nightlife Hub

Northbridge is known as *the* place to head out on a Friday or Saturday night. Much of the action focuses on the bar and club scene, which keeps going until the small hours. A range of tastes is catered for, from funk and jazz at the **Universal Bar** to serious dance tunes at **The Deen**. But if finding your way past boozy young things isn't your scene, perhaps go for dinner at one of the many restaurants and head home before things start to get messy around midnight. Northbridge has also been known for violence on these nights, but there is a strong police presence, and you generally won't find much trouble.

SEE ALSO MUSIC AND DANCE, P.81; NIGHTLIFE, P.85

The **Performing Arts Centre Society** (PACS) ③, occupies a former school. The soaring main gallery has studios on a mezzanine, and there's a bar-cum-café and a performance theatre on the ground floor. Sharing space with PACS are the **Photographers Gallery**, **WA Actors Centre** and **Impressions Gallery**, which shows prints. **Artrage**, Perth's alternative arts coordinator, is around the corner.

Across the concourse, the **Battye State Library** contains the state archives, film and photographs. The main attraction for casual visitors is likely to be the discard bookshop in the front lobby.

The black-and-white sculpture *Coalesce*, by Akio Makigawa, in front of the library, has become a popular meeting place; the stepped forms symbolise the stages of acquiring knowledge.

SEE ALSO THEATRE, P.116

The Western Australian Museum

Next to the Battye building is the **Western Australian Museum** ④, an elegant red-brick and sandstone building with a colonnaded upper floor. In WA, scientists have access to some of the oldest land on Earth and its earliest life forms, not to mention evidence of the life of early man, such as rock

Below: investigate fossils at the Western Australian Museum.

In the **Blue Room** at the **Performing Arts Centre Society** around 20 shows a year are put on by the writers, directors, actors, technicians and managers who create them. Each show runs for a two- to three-week season. *See Theatre, p.116.*

Subiaco

Subiaco is a suburb that has it all, cool shops, top restaurants, great culture, major sports grounds and a lively vibe. Creative industries such as advertising, publishing and design tend to be based here, and housing prices certainly indicate that Subiaco is one of the most desirable addresses in Perth. Much of the residential architecture is cottage-style, or bungalows, but many original homes have been restored and extended, and make for impressive viewing. As a visitor, Saturday lunch or brunch can be combined with a look around the ever-popular Station Street Markets and some up-market shopping or a visit to the theatre.

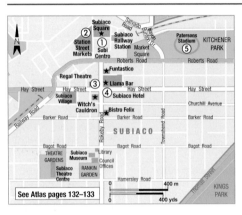

See Atlas pages 132–133

Above: buy a new hat while shopping in the market.

On the Ground

Subiaco Station was sunk below ground in 1998 in a daring piece of planning designed to create the spectacular **Subi Centro** ①, a complex of houses, apartments and offices that has transformed the area.

From the top of Rokeby Road, it is a 15-minute walk to the Saw Avenue entrance to Kings Park, which has 400 hectares (1,000 acres) of natural bush, as well as lakes, lawns, children's playgrounds and botanical gardens. Walking is easy, but bicycles can be hired from a kiosk in the Fraser Avenue car park for longer explorations.

To rejuvenate the north, the rail line had to go. The process of sinking it during the 1990s was complex and controversial, but what the America's Cup did for Fremantle, Subi Centro has done for Subiaco. Drab, empty factories were replaced by smart apartments, offices and restaurants. The station square is spotless, and the electric trains, unseen, glide noiselessly in and out. For WA the concept of creating a new urban space by pushing the rail underground was revolutionary.

Markets and Theatres

On the western side of Subiaco Square are **Station Street Markets** ②. This covered market is a Perth institution that has somehow survived the gentrification all around. A redevelopment project, completed in 2008, made the markets more compact. Local people still come here every weekend to browse the 50-odd stalls selling everything from giftware to freshly baked goodies and exotic fruit and vegetables grown by local families.

The hub of Subiaco lies at the Rokeby/Hay crossroads. The Subiaco Hotel faces the **Regal Theatre** ③, neighbours since the 1930s. The Regal opened as a 'hard-top' cinema in 1938, replacing the open-air Coliseum Picture Garden, one of many in its

Left: bountiful produce on offer at the Station Street Markets.

are interspersed with several notable and popular restaurants, such as **Funtastico** and **Bistro Felix**.

SEE ALSO RESTAURANTS, P.105–6

Football Fans

Subiaco is also home to the **Patersons Stadium** ⑤ (formerly Subiaco Oval), WA's headquarters of AFL (Australian Football League), otherwise known as Aussie Rules, the unique Australian game. The Oval is also the home base and grand final venue for the Western Australian Football League, as well as being the home ground of local WAFL side, simply called 'Subiaco'.

In the long winter season there is an AFL match every week, plus WAFL matches at the Oval and elsewhere. A striking example of sporting architecture, the Oval has all-seater modern stands with a capacity of 43,000. The AFL teams in Perth are the West Coast Eagles (who have won the premiership several times) and the Fremantle Dockers (who align themselves as a 'working-class' side, although their fans are usually anything but). You'll know if a game is being played, as the roar of the crowd can be heard kilometres away.

SEE ALSO SPORTS, P.112

time. While many Subiaco theatres closed down, the trend was reversed at the Regal, where live performance replaced film in 1977.

The interior of the Regal is as stunning as the Art Deco exterior. The original chrome-and-jarrah fittings are still in place, as is Paddy's Bar (and his chair), named after Paddy Baker, who bought the cinema in 1946. Paddy also installed the love seat in the balcony, as well as the 'Crying Room', so that mothers could attend to their offspring while still watching the show. Paddy died in 1986, leaving his beloved building to the people of WA. The Regal is now listed with the National Trust.

Also on the Rokeby/Hay crossroads is the **Subiaco Hotel** ④, which has been transformed from a standard pub into a cosmopolitan entertainment spot, with an award-winning restaurant. **The Llama Bar** (opposite the Regal) is owned by the same proprietors and hits the same high standards.

SEE ALSO FOOD AND DRINK, P.61; PUBS AND BARS, P.98; RESTAURANTS, P.105; SHOPPING, P.110; THEATRE P.117

Commercial Hub

At the last count Subiaco had over 100 cafés and restaurants, homeware stores, health and beauty outlets, jewellery stores and bookstores. Stylish shops

Right: the Subiaco Hotel.

Fremantle

The port city of Fremantle, which lies 19km (12 miles) from Perth, is an intriguing mix. Known as a laid-back place, where long-standing hippies rub shoulders with young up-and-comers, Fremantle has become a residence of choice since it hosted the America's Cup in the 1980s and hit the map. Now, property prices are soaring in this former working-class and artists' enclave; the main street is even known as 'the cappuccino strip', where everyone heads for a pavement seat to spot and be spotted. Watch boy racers cruising past, while locals walk their organic fruit and vegetables home from the markets and visitors soak up the relaxed atmosphere.

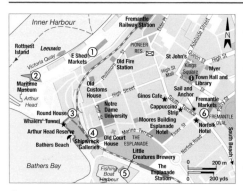

About Fremantle

Freo, as it is known locally, has a friendly, confident feel and a Mediterranean flavour. Artists have thrived here for years, with generations of writers, actors, painters, musicians and craft workers finding inspiration and low-cost studios in the old port buildings. Artists were initially drawn to the area as it was away from the busy, business-focused attitude of Perth, and even now, living in Fremantle can get you labelled as a 'Freo hippie'. Now, of course, to own property in Freo, you would have to be a very well-heeled hippie.

Fremantle Port is WA's main port, and shifts an enormous amount of cargo each week, yet is noticeably clean, with colourful mountains of containers and gantries. Even the distant oil-storage tanks look scrubbed white and silver. Day and night, cargo containers waiting clearance to enter and unload linger off the coast near Rottnest Island.

Around the Quay

The quay is also a departure point for the ferry to **Rottnest Island**, as well as the location for the main maritime sights and the **E Shed Markets** ①, an eclectic collection of Australiana, diving gear, clothing and generic gift stores. There's also a family-friendly food court that stays open until 8pm on weekends.

Right: relaxing on 'the cappuccino strip'.

At the far end of the quay you will see the modern, sail-like roof of the **Maritime Museum** ②, an imaginatively executed exploration of Fremantle's many and varied maritime industries. Even if maritime exhibits are not of interest to you, it is worth a visit just to admire the exceptional architecture.

A short walk from Victoria Quay is Arthur Head, site of the **Round House** ③. This is WA's oldest public building and its first gaol, built in 1830, where Captain Fremantle landed to claim Western Australia for the British Crown. WA's prison populace soon outgrew the capacity of the Round House and its eight small cells. A series of bigger prisons replaced it, but the Round House was used as a police lock-up until 1900.

Left: fishing in Fremantle Harbour, with the Maritime Museum in the distance.

North of the brewery and boatyards, a host of restaurants, ice-cream parlours and cafés line the Fishing Boat Harbour, a working harbour for a 500-strong fleet. From here, head up Essex Street, which leads to South Terrace, known as **'the cappuccino strip'**. Along with good coffee (the best is arguably at local institution, **Gino's**), you'll also find some of the best beer. The **Sail and Anchor** boutique pub brewery serves many excellent brews.

First opened as a market hall in 1897 and now splendidly restored, **Fremantle Markets** ⑥ is National Trust-listed. Spread across more than 150 stalls you'll find fresh fish and crustaceans, fruit and vegetables, cheeses, freshly baked bread, coffees, herbs, spices and health foods. Crafts and Australiana also abound: sheepskin and leather goods, jarrah and cane products, dried flowers, opals, local shells and pottery.

SEE ALSO CAFÉS P.35; FOOD AND DRINK, P.60; HOTELS, P.71; PUBS AND BARS, P.98–9; SHOPPING, P.110

Below the jail is **Whalers' Tunnel**, cut through the rock in 1837 to connect Bathers Beach and the jetty with the settlement. Hunters of the Fremantle Whaling Company used to drag their kill through the tunnel, and it is the only remnant of the whaling industry that was so crucial to the young colony.

From here, walk along Cliff Street (right off the High Street). At the end is the original WA Maritime Museum, now known as the **Shipwreck**

Galleries ④, devoted to marine archaeology. Treasures from the *Batavia*, a famous Dutch shipwreck, are on display alongside relics from other ancient wrecks.

SEE ALSO EXCURSIONS, P.46; MUSEUMS AND GALLERIES, P.78–9

The Esplanade and South Terrace

From the Shipwreck Galleries, proceed along Marine Terrace to reach the prominent **Esplanade Hotel**. Modern extensions are well blended into the original facade, built in 1890s gold-rush style like many Fremantle hotels. One of the main attractions is the harbour-side **Little Creatures Brewery** ⑤ whose output is sold around the state and widely exported. Little Creatures is also a busy restaurant and bar, famous for alternative staff, pizzas, handmade fries, and huge warehouse-style dining area. It's always busy and always good fun.

> If you visit South Beach (at the end of South Terrace) you will notice a statue out in the water. It depicts the famous WA engineer C.Y. O'Connor, who designed the port of Fremantle and also the pipeline responsible for taking water out to Kalgoorlie and the goldfields. Sadly for C.Y., he suffered so much abuse over the pipeline that he rode his horse out from South Beach and shot himself. The pipeline was completed after his death and is considered an engineering masterpiece.

Cottesloe, Claremont, Swanbourne and Scarborough

T he Perth area is blessed with some beautiful coastline, and there are multiple choices when it comes to where to visit. Scarborough has one of the best metro surf breaks, while Swanbourne is great if you want a full body tan without bather marks. Meanwhile, the western suburbs of Cottesloe and Claremont are home to some of Perth's most fabulous folk.

For the ultimate Perth 'Sunday session' head to the **Ocean Beach Hotel** (OBH). Perched across the road from North Cottesloe Beach, the OBH attracts a young crowd, often from the countryside. In hot weather the large windows are opened, and you can enjoy getting a tan while you drink a 'middie' of beer and watch the sun set. Also legendary for its Sunday drinking session is the Cottesloe Hotel, where, if you miss out on prime real estate near the front of the bar, you can enjoy the party at mosphere in the revamped rear courtyard. See also *Pubs and Bars, p.99.*

Cottesloe

Cottesloe is a trendy beach-side suburb with some of Australia's most spectacular views and highest property prices. A million dollars won't get you much of a house here, but using the beautiful beaches and hanging out is free. Locals do it in droves and it is equally popular with visitors.

Dominating the beach front is the graceful outline of the **Indiana Tea House** ①, an elegant, colonial-style restaurant housed in a wooden pavilion right on the beach.

It's a good place for a coffee while watching the sparkling Indian Ocean. The bars and cafés that line Marine Parade are set slightly back from the water, but they enjoy great ocean views and fling open their windows to let patrons make the most of them. On a hot summer's day the lively atmosphere floats out onto the street.

Cottesloe Beach ② is great for swimming, especially in the summer, when surfing is banned except beyond the groyne. Land-

scaped lawns rise up behind the beach, lined with Norfolk pines, whose distinctive shape helps lend Cottesloe its character and provide sunbathers with some much-needed shade.

If the crowds become too much, **North Cottesloe Beach** ③ is far quieter, and only a minute's drive along Marine Parade or a short walk along the beach away from Cottesloe. There are no facilities and the beach is unpatrolled, but consequently much more peaceful.
SEE ALSO BEACHES, P.28, 29

Left: wine and good food at The Blue Duck, Cottesloe *(see Cafés, p.35)*.

Swanbourne Beach backs onto the SAS (Special Air Service) army base. There is a firing range which is often used, so if you hear the cracks of gunfire, don't panic, it is just the SAS practising their aim.

the West Coast Highway, from which several beautiful beaches can be accessed, including **City Beach**, **Floreat Beach** and **Brighton Beach**.

Scarborough Beach ⑥ is the most developed of the beaches in the Perth area. Offering a wide range of waterfront accommodation, it's a popular choice for holidaymakers who prefer to base themselves outside the city centre, as well as very popular with surfers taking advantage of the great breaks on offer.

The beach-front jogging track is always in use by keep-fit fanatics, while for those who prefer a more sedate pace there's the Scarborough Beach to Trigg Beach Heritage Walk. **Trigg Beach** ⑦ is one of Perth's most popular surf spots and also has a popular snorkelling area, Mettams Pool, which is to the north of the main surf/swim area.

SEE ALSO BEACHES, P.28–31

Claremont

Claremont is a neighbouring suburb – it doesn't have Cottesloe's beach frontage but it does have Swan River access. Claremont is known for the stylish shops on Bayview Terrace and St Quentin's Avenue. Here you'll find the glamorous new **Claremont Quarter** ④ – a designer retail precinct that's home to David Jones, Country Road's flagship Western Australian store, with men's, women's, children's and homewares sections, and a host of Australian designer boutiques including Sass & Bide, Alannah Hill and Carla Zampatti. On Bayview Terrace you will find the fabulous shoe store, Zomp, and other popular brands.

When you tire of shopping, there are several great eating options on 'the terrace' and

throughout the precinct.
SEE ALSO FASHION, P.52

Swanbourne to Scarborough

North of Cottesloe is **Swanbourne Beach** ⑤, which is best-known for its nudist bathing on the far side of the dunes. Situated right next to a military base and accessed by a no-through-road, it has plenty of privacy, but swimming conditions can be rough.

Following the road around the back of the army barracks, you soon hit the start of

Right: surfing is very popular at Perth's beaches.

Swan Valley and the Perth Hills

The Swan Valley and Perth Hills are just short drives from the city centre, yet once there, you feel as if you are miles away and, in some cases, that you have stepped back in time. It is one of Perth's perks that it is a small enough city to enable easy access to the distinctive Australian landscape around it. Both the Swan Valley and the Perth Hills areas have wonderful villages with great atmospheres, plentiful bushland and lots of fine food and wine to tempt you away from the big city.

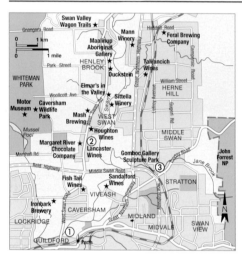

The Swan Valley

If there is only time for one longer excursion, a trip to **Guildford** ① is arguably the one to make. It is only 30 minutes away by train or road from the CBD, and a further five minutes by car will take you through the vineyards of WA's oldest wine area, where wineries, breweries, restaurants and tourist attractions welcome visitors through the year.

Guildford is actually considered a suburb of Perth and is easily explored on foot. Close to the train station, the award-winning Visitor Centre can provide a map of short walking trails taking from 20 minutes to an hour. Opposite the station, a parade of antiques shops line James Street between the enormous Federation-style **Guildford Hotel** (c. 1900) and the Art Deco **Town Hall**.

Sweet Treats

With a number of excellent wineries lining the Swan Valley region, visitors often concentrate their tour on comparing as many wines as possible, but along the trail are dozens more attractions. A sweet one is the **Margaret River Chocolate Company**, near **Lancaster Wines** ②. It sells all kinds of delicious confections, such as hand-made truffles, hot drinks, sauces, cakes, novelties and chocolate bars, and it also offers free chocolate-tastings.

Swan Valley Wagon Trails transports visitors in pioneer-style covered wagons, drawn by Clydesdale horses, through the olive groves and pine forests of the region. Tours vary and can be tailor-made for vineyard tours, evening trips and to meet wine cruises from Perth.
SEE ALSO WINE COUNTRY, P.126–7

German Brews

Along West Swan Road's gastronomic trail, a pair of German-style microbreweries, **Elmar's in the Valley** and **Duckstein**, each make their

A few kilometres along the Great Eastern Highway is the road to **Mundaring Weir** *(see picture, right)* which is an impressive sight, even though it is nowhere near capacity due to years of drought. You can walk across the weir, and there is a museum on site.

Left: the Guildford Hotel.

In September it's time for Spring in the Valley. Held across a weekend, wineries are the focus for visitors to the valley. You will see bus-loads of cheerful folk tasting wines, and probably not spitting them out often enough. It is a fun weekend, however, and worth visiting the valley during this time.

lie along the Great Eastern Highway, about 7km (4 miles) from Guildford.
SEE ALSO PARKS, P.93

Kalamunda

At **Kalamunda** ⑥, early European settlement of the region can be explored at the **History Village**. It has an original post office dating from 1901, the district's first state school, a settler's cottage, workshops and two railway stations, all equipped with original artefacts and furnishings.

Kalamunda is also the starting point for another round of wineries, this time in the **Bickley Valley**. Elevated conditions on the Darling Scarp have produced a cluster of award-winning boutique vineyards, such as **Piesse Brook** and **Hainault**.

beer according to the 'Bavarian Purity Law' of 1516. Only pure water, malt and hops are used. Other breweries include Feral Brewing Co., Ironbark Brewery and Mash Brewing. Good food can also be found at most of the breweries in the valley.
SEE ALSO PUBS AND BARS, P.99

Arts and Crafts

Several wineries have galleries, but the best selection of paintings, sculpture and

Below: Mundaring Weir.

souvenirs are sold in specialist galleries such as **Gomboc Gallery Sculpture Park** ③ in Middle Swan, the southern hemisphere's largest gallery, much of it devoted to outdoor sculpture. Another is the **Maalinup Aboriginal Gallery**. Operated by local Nyungar people, it also offers evening entertainments, storytelling, didgeridoo-playing and bush food-tastings.

Into the Perth Hills

Driving in WA is easy going, even in the Swan Valley with all its tourist attractions. Driving through the hills of the **Darling Range** is more leisurely still. Like the growing number of commuters living on the semi-rural fringes of Perth, visitors can enjoy speedy access to small towns such as Kalamunda and Jarrahdale, and natural attractions such as **Mundaring Weir** ④ and **John Forrest National Park** ⑤. Entrances

A–Z

In the following section Perth's attractions and services are organised by theme, under alphabetical headings. Items that link to another theme are cross-referenced. All sights that fall within the atlas section at the end of the book are given a page number and grid reference.

Aboriginal Culture

Perth's Aboriginal peoples suffered displacement for years after European settlement, like much of Australia's indigenous population, and it is only recently that some ground has begun to be made up. In 2008, the newly elected prime minister, Kevin Rudd, made a national public apology to the Stolen Generation. There are many sites of recognised profound significance to Aboriginal people in Perth, and increasingly Noongar history and culture is being given a voice in the city's museums and galleries.

Perth's Indigenous History

Perth's indigenous population, now known collectively as **Noongar** (also spelt Nyungar) people, belong to the southwest corner of Western Australia. Before the Europeans arrived in 1829, they were divided into 13 separate tribes. They obeyed the mythical laws of the Dreaming, a philosophy that closely connected them to the land.

When white settlers arrived, tribal numbers were depleted by disease and bloody confrontations with the Europeans, including the 1834 'Battle of Pinjarra'. Although the Europeans had initially traded amicably with Noongar people, rifts developed when local tribes were declared as British subjects and sacred land was seized.

As more and more land in the region was turned over to farming, most Aboriginal people were forced into towns or camps. From 1890 to 1958, the Native Welfare Act removed children of indigenous descent from their biological parents, especially children of mixed European and Aboriginal descent. Many Noongar children became part of this 'Stolen Generation' after being forcibly removed from their homes and placed in camps at Carrolup and Moore River. It is estimated that up to 25 percent of Noongar children were sent to these concentration camps.

In the latter decades of the 20th century, past wrongs such as these began to be recognised. Pressure to recognise Aboriginal land rights mounted, culminating in 1992, with the High Court Mabo ruling, acknowledging Aboriginal rights to some traditional lands. This was ratified a year later with the Native Title Act, which has resulted in many long and tortuous claims passing through the courts. Meanwhile the book and film ***Rabbit-Proof Fence***, based on the true story of three girls who escaped from an Aboriginal camp during the 1930s, garnered international acclaim and attention.
SEE ALSO FILM, P.56

Rottnest Island

In 1839, Rottnest Island became a penal establishment for indigenous people. Over 3,700 men and boys, most of them Noongar, were imprisoned there for offences such as burning bush or digging up vegetables on their own land. There are believed to be at least 369 indigenous people buried on Rottnest Island. In 1904 the prison was closed, and in 1917 the island was declared an A-Class Reserve, ensuring land could not be leased or sold.

The island is known as 'Wadjemup' to Aboriginals, and has great spiritual significance to them. Following the appearance of a dead whale on a Rottnest beach in December 2005, Aboriginal

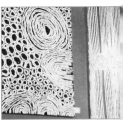

Right: Aboriginal artworks.

Left: Noongar Aboriginals celebrate their native land title win in 2006.

One of Australia's top Aboriginal theatre companies is based in Perth. **Yirra Yaakin**, meaning 'stand tall' in the Noongar language, began with a youth theatre project in 1993 and has grown into an impressive, award-winning theatre company. They focus not only on creating important theatre, but also keeping Aboriginal performing arts determined by Aboriginal people. If you can catch a play while you are in Perth, it is worth it. *See Theatre, p.117.*

elders believe the island is slowly reawakening after its dark years as a prison.

Walking tours, run by knowledgeable volunteer guides, depart daily from the island's Visitor Centre. They cover a range of subjects from Aboriginal history on the island to environmental issues (most are free; some have a small charge).

Aboriginal Art

Aboriginal Art Gallery
Fraser Avenue, Kings Park; tel: 08-9481 7082; www.aboriginalgallery.com.au; Mon–Fri 10.30am–4.30pm, Sat–Sun 11am–4pm; free; bus: 37, 39; map p.133 D1
Sells fine indigenous arts and crafts. It usually has an Aboriginal artist in residence and

has a look-out point above.
The Art Gallery of WA
Perth Cultural Centre, 47 James Street; tel: 08-9492 6622; www.artgallery.wa.gov.au; Mon–Wed 10am–5pm; free; train: Perth City; map p.134 B3
On the first floor of the main building, two galleries house one of the continent's best collections of Aboriginal art, comprising paintings, bark paintings and carvings giving a comprehensive overview of traditional and contemporary works from Arnhemland, the Central Desert and Western Australia.
SEE ALSO MUSEUMS AND GALLERIES, P.76
Indigenart, at the Mossenson Galleries
115 Hay Street, Subiaco; tel: 08-9388 2899; www.indigenart.com.au; Mon–Fri 10am–5pm, Sat 11am–4pm; free; train: Subiaco; map p.135 D1
Indigenart represents a wide range of Aboriginal artists from around Australia, and the quality of work is very high.
Japingka Gallery
47 High Street, Fremantle; tel: 08-9335 8265; www.japingka.

com.au; Mon–Fri 10am–5.30pm, Sat 10am–5pm, Sun noon–5pm; free; train: Fremantle
Specialises in paintings and limited-edition prints by Aboriginal artists, with exhibitions of the works of specific artists and communities changing every six weeks. Contemporary Aboriginal artists of all styles and major Australian regions feature. The ground-floor gallery includes paintings, prints, works on paper, didgeridoos, books and artefacts, and an exclusive range of hand-tufted pure-wool rugs with designs by Jimmy Pike and Doris Gingingara.

Tours

Indigenous Heritage Tours
Kings Park; book through WA Visitor Centre, tel: 08-9483 1111 or the Aboriginal Art Gallery, tel: 08-9481 7082; www.indigenouswa.com; daily 1.30pm; admission charge; bus: 37, 39; map p.134 A2
Run by an Aboriginal guide, the 90-minute tours depart daily from the Wadjuk car park, opposite the entry to the Botanic Garden.

Beaches

Western Australians are proud of their coastline, and rightly so. In a state dominated by dry deserts, the sparkling waters of the Indian Ocean exert an almost hypnotic appeal. For locals, whether gathering with friends for a picnic or taking an early morning constitutional along the shore, the beach is a focal point, especially in summer. It can be hard to tell when one beach has turned into another, as they all merge seamlessly into one, but there are signposts in every parking spot identifying the beach, the surf and swimming conditions, and the available facilities, invaluable information if you are visiting an unpatrolled stretch.

Brighton Beach

Train: Clarkson, then bus: 400
Brighton Beach is a good-sized stretch of sand, framed by attractively landscaped picnic and playground areas. Access is just a short walk from the large car park through the dunes. Lifeguards are on patrol, surfers have their own designated area indicated by blue-and-white signs, and there is a kiosk for refreshments. Primarily, Brighton is a good alternative for those who prefer to be near the attractions and amenities of Scarborough, but without the crowds.

City Beach

Bus: 84
Situated about 12km (7.5 miles) from Perth, City Beach is the name of a suburb as well as the beach. A large grassy area slopes gently down to a wide stretch of sand overlooked by the Surf Life Saving Club. Toilets, a kiosk serving refreshments, and gas barbecue facilities mean you can spend a day here quite comfortably, morning until late. There are also volleyball nets on the sand and a playground for the kids. Parking is plentiful.

Cottesloe Beach

www.cottesloebeach.com; bus: 102; train: Cottesloe
Trains run out to Cottesloe from the city centre. To get to the beach from the station, cross over the railway line, head down Jarrad Street and turn right onto Marine Parade. If you want to investigate Cottesloe's Napoleon Street the station is located at the

Left: getting the boats out at Leighton Beach.

Left: using sun protection is essential in Australia.

In the height of summer, the sun is exceptionally fierce. To avoid sunburn, visit the beach early in the morning, and try not to spend too much time in the sun. Sunscreen, hats and sunglasses are essential. Most people, unprotected, will start to burn in less than 15 minutes. A burn from the Australian sun is like no other, and you can expect a lot of pain, a lot of heat and possibly peeling and even blistering. If you want the bronzed look, a good spray tan is the smart option. Beauty salons all around Perth can help out.

end of the small but trendy shopping strip.

On Marine Parade you'll also find several cafés which are happy to take in sandy-footed customers, as well as a surf shop, where you can hire surfboards and purchase clothing and thongs (flip-flops, the essential Australian footwear).

Most of the beach action takes place on the sand in front of the **Indiana Tea House**, where the lifeguards keep a watchful eye. Swimming conditions are generally good here, and surfboards are banned during the height of summer (Oct–Mar), so swimmers have the water to themselves. Surfing is allowed on the artificial reef on the other side of the groyne. Lots of families come here as facilities are good – there are toilets, picnic benches, barbecues, a children's playground and plenty of room for children to run around. At night, make the most of the floodlit beach and enjoy fish and chips down on the sand.

Floreat Beach

Bus: 81, 84, 91

In the lovely, affluent suburb of the same name is a large, attractive beach that is particularly popular with locals. It is patrolled only part-time, so be sure to look out for the red-and-yellow flags. There is a good range of amenities, including toilets, plenty of parking, free public volleyball courts, a café, kiosk and large children's playground set under

brightly coloured shades on a grassed picnic area.

North Cottesloe Beach

Bus: 102 to Forrest Street; train: Cottesloe

North Cottesloe is quieter than the main beach, yet is only a few hundred metres away. Road-side parking is limited, but you could leave your car at Cottesloe and walk. The beach is unpatrolled, so you swim at your

Below: the sundial at Cottesloe Beach.

Left: lunch at The Little Starfish Café, South Beach.

Scarborough is certainly the largest and most developed beach destination in the Perth area. A good selection of accommodation in the area caters to holidaymakers who prefer to be near the beach, while prime breakers on this part of the coast mean it is a focal point for local surfers. The beach is patrolled, and regular surf life-saving competitions and displays are held here, making for entertaining viewing.

All types of water sports are available, including kite-surfing and windsurfing, or you can just sit back and watch the fun from the grassed picnic area behind the dunes.

Sorrento Beach and Hillary's Boat Harbour

Train: Stirling, then bus: 423 to Hillary's Boat Harbour

With plenty of beach-side accommodation and the shops, cafés and attractions of Hillary's Boat Harbour right next door, Sorrento is a good place to come for the day. Should you tire of the wide expanse of sand and sparkling ocean, you can easily walk across the car park to Hillary's for a bite to eat or a browse among the shops. Sorrento itself has a beach-side kiosk and toilets, and is patrolled by life-savers, as winds can sometimes make conditions rough.

People with very small children should avoid the surf beaches and go instead to Hillary's Boat Harbour. Despite its name, boats are actually prohibited in some parts of the marina, allowing for safe swimming in the flat calm of the harbour. The small man-made beach is

It can be hard to know which beach to choose, especially when they merge into one long swath. The following guidelines should help.

For families:
Cottesloe, Mettam's Pool, Hamersley Pool, Hillary's Boat Harbour.

For water sports:
Scarborough and Trigg are best for surfing, and Leighton and Port Beach for parasailing, windsurfing and kite-surfing.

For snorkelling/diving:
Marmion Marine Park (join an organised trip from Hillary's Boat Harbour).

For the best après beach:
Cottesloe and Scarborough.

For nudists:
Swanbourne, north of Cottesloe, has a strip for nudists near the dunes at the northern end.

For rock pools:
Bennion Beach, Watermans Beach.

For dogs:
Whitfords Beach has a dog beach (and an area for horses), with a weekend dog-wash service. Port and Leighton and South Beach are good, too.

own risk. In a prime location overlooking the water are **The Blue Duck** and **Barchetta** cafés, with balcony views out to **Rottnest Island**.
SEE ALSO CAFÉS, P.35; EXCURSIONS, P.46

Port Beach and Leighton Beach

Bus: 103 to Queen Victoria Street

Port and Leighton run into each other. Strong winds pretty much rule out sunbathing in the afternoons, and a sign warns swimmers of strong currents and submerged rocks at Port, but this is a good spot to watch parasailing. Home of the Fremantle Surf Life Saving Club, Leighton Beach is also best-suited to wind- and kite-surfing, as strong currents and submerged rocks make swimming risky. There is a small car park and a kiosk. It is a very popular beach for dog walking, too.

Scarborough Beach

Train: Glendalough, then bus: 400 to Scarborough

always busy with families, many of whom turn up early and set up camp for the day under one of the brightly coloured canvases that provide shade here. There's an adventure playground on the sand itself, while further back from the beach is a small funfair, water slides, mini golf and trampolines. The beach is patrolled, but conditions are so tame that residents bring their children here for swimming lessons.

The surrounding precinct is filled with boutiques, souvenir shops, bars and restaurants, most of which line the timber boardwalk known as Sorrento Quay.

South Beach

Train: Fremantle, then walk 100m/yds south to Phillimore Street, take the CAT bus to South Terrace, then walk 700m/yds to South Beach
You will cross a train track and see a large grassed area before you see the water. South Beach is the most popular of the southern beaches in the Perth area. Owing to its proximity to Fremantle, it often gets overlooked, as most people come to Fremantle to shop in the markets or catch a ferry to Rottnest Island, not to swim. However, South Beach is a real find, and is also a stop on the free CAT bus as it loops around town. There is a kiosk. the Pickled Fig Café, barbecue facilities, toilets, children's playground, good parking and a grassy area for games. This is also another popular beach for dog walking.

South Cottesloe

Bus: 102; train: Mosman Park
South Cottesloe Beach has a children's playground on a grassed area set back from

the beach, but is otherwise lacking in amenities. All the facilities of Cottesloe, however, are a stone's throw away, so if you like to lose the crowds but not venture too far from facilities, this is a good spot. Access to the beach is again by steps only, although you can walk back along the sand to Cottesloe itself.

Swanbourne

Bus: 102, stop after North Street
North of Cottesloe, Swanbourne is best known for nudist bathing on the far side of the dunes. Situated right next to a military base and accessed by a no-through road, it has plenty of privacy, but swimming conditions can be rough. However, if this is your top pick, you are probably here for sunbathing rather than swimming. There are toilets, the Naked Fig Café, which overlooks a large grassy playground area, and lots of parking.

Trigg Beach

Train: Glendalough, then bus: 408 to Scarborough, then bus: 458 to Karrinyup Road

Trigg Beach is another popular spot with surfers and sailboarders. The beach is patrolled, but strong rips often develop and can make swimming dangerous, so it is the place for those proficient in the water. As at Cottesloe, there's a good choice of bars, cafés and restaurants, and a supermarket just a short walk away. On Sundays the bars can get a little rowdy as the legendary 'Sunday session' kicks off in the late afternoon, so if you're not up for partying, it's best to stay away. Clarko Reserve, a big grassed area back from the beach, has picnic tables, barbecues and a children's playground.

Watermans Beach

Train: Warwick, then bus 423 to Cliff Street
Watermans has a good stretch of sand and interesting rock pools to explore. The water is calm in the shallows, making it good for children and inexperienced swimmers, and there's a children's playground next to the beach under the shade of the Norfolk pines.

Below: surfing and sailing in the sparkling seas.

Cafés

It sometimes appears that no one in Perth actually has a job, as the cafés here always appear to be full, no matter what day of the week or what time of day it is. Relaxing at a café at the weekend with the paper, family and dog in tow is a popular pastime, as is the local activity of people-watching, most common in areas such as Fremantle, Leederville and the city centre. Coffee in Perth is taken very seriously, and the food served also tends to be fresh and of good quality, although prices can vary dramatically. For further listings of places to eat, see *Pubs and Bars, p.96–9,* and *Restaurants, p.100–7.*

Swan River and Kings Park

Old Brewery Café Restaurant

173 Mounts Bay Road, Crawley; tel: 08-9211 8999; www.theold brewery.com.au; daily 7.30am–late; bus: 102; map p.137 D4

Enjoy Swan River views and a crafted beer from the on-site microbrewery. There are plenty of interesting dishes on the menu, such as cumin-spiced lamb cutlets, beetroot couscous and tahini mayo. The venue is flexible, so you could enjoy a three-course meal or just a light breakfast and coffee followed by a stroll along the river banks.

City Centre

No. 44 King Street

44 King Street; tel: 08-9321 4476; daily 7am–late; train: Perth; map p.134 A2

With a menu that changes daily, this is a Perth eating institution where you will find businesspeople sealing deals over breakfast, locals popping in for a coffee and couples dining at night on a special occasion. The lofty, semi-industrial space allows you to watch baristas, chefs and bakers at work, or you can simply gaze out onto the city's most fashionable street and people-watch. There is a large and interesting wine list.

The Cheeky Sparrow

1/317 Murray Street; tel: 08-9486 4947; www.cheekysparrow.com.au; Mon–Sat 7am–midnight; train: Perth; map p.134 A2

Also on Wolfe Lane, this is a warm, quirky and super-chic spot for breakfast, lunch, coffee, shared plates and a drink.

Etro

49 King Street; tel: 08-9481 1148; www.etro.com.au; daily 7am–5pm, Fri dinner from 6pm; bus: red CAT; map p.134 A2

In good weather you will always find Etro's footpath seating jammed with trendy young things sipping strong coffees. Inside you can enjoy well-priced cooked breakfasts and a large range of tasty lunches and dinners.

Tiger, Tiger

Shop 4/329 Murray Street; tel: 08-9322 8055; www.tigertigercoffeebar.com;

Most cafés and restaurants in Perth take last orders for dinner around 9pm, so even when people say they are open 'late' this often means orders will be taken and then you are welcome to stay as long as you like after that. If you are keen on a late sitting, make sure you call ahead and ask what time the kitchen closes. If in doubt, book a table on popular nights.

Mon 7am–5pm, Tue–Wed 7am–8pm, Thur 7am–9pm, Fri 7am–midnight, Sat 7.45am–5pm; train: Perth; bus: red CAT; map p.134 A2

Located off Wolfe Lane, one of the city's revitalised laneways, this ultra cool café/bar draws a hip crowd and serves seriously good coffee and wine.

Leederville

Cranked Coffee

Shop 5, 106 Oxford Street; tel: 08-6161 0730; www.cranked.net.au; Mon–Fri 6.30am–4pm, Sat 7.30am–4pm, Sun 8am–4pm; train: Leederville

Located opposite the Leederville train station, this family

Left: Perth's cafés offer everything from a proper Aussie breakfast, complete with vegemite, to light bites at sundown **(bottom right)**.

friendly diner is a great place to relax alfresco with a cup of steaming fair trade coffee or casual tapas while the kids play on the grass in front of the café.

Little Caesars Pizzeria
127 Oxford Street; tel: 08-9444 0499; www.littlecaesars pizzeria.com.au; Sun–Thur 5pm–late, Fri–Sat 11.30am–late; train: Leederville
Award-winning Little Caesars is renowned for making not just Perth's best pizza, but the whole world's. In 2010 owner Theo Kalogeracos won the title of World Champion Pizza Maker at the Las Vegas Pizza Show. Grab a slice and settle into the bustling diner to see what all the fuss is about. There is another branch at Hillary's Boat Harbour, tel: 08-9243 3114.

Sayers Food
1/224 Carr Place; tel: 08-9227 0429; www.sayersfood.com.au; daily 7am–5pm, Thur until 9pm; train: Leederville
Do battle for a table at this funky café which serves tasty, fresh cuisine. There are ever-changing menus at the counter, plus a cabinet of treats such as goat's-cheese tarts, salmon roulade and home-baked cakes.

Northbridge

Beaufort Street Merchant
488 Beaufort Street, Highgate; tel: 08-9328 6299; www.beaufortmerchant.com; daily 7am–late public holidays 8am–late; bus: 21
Fine wine store, gourmet providore, delicatessen and funky brasserie – the Beaufort Street Merchant in the up and coming district of Highgate, is all of these, and serves some of the best coffee north of the CBD.

Little Willy's
267 William Street; Mon–Fri 6am–3pm; train: Perth; bus: blue CAT; map p.134 A3
Up beat and friendly with a laid-back atmosphere, this pocket-sized gem in the heart of Northbridge offers tasty, unpretentious food and truly great coffee. It's one of Perth's best-kept secrets.

The Moon Café
323 William Street; tel: 08-9328 7474; www.themoon.com.au; Mon–Tue 6pm–1am, Wed–Thur and Sun 11am–1am, Fri–Sat 11am–3.30am; train: Perth; bus: blue CAT; map p.134 B3
Northbridge's best-loved late night café, "The Moon" is an alternative urban lounge popular with students and night owls. Its meals are very well priced and it's a great spot for a quiet drink before heading out into Northbridge.

Tarts Café and Home Providore
212 Lake Street; tel: 08-9328 6607; www.tartscafe.com.au; daily 7am–3pm; bus: blue CAT; map p.134 B4
Nestled amongst the terraced homes on Lake Street. For breakfast, try the scrambled eggs with feta, wilted spinach, oven-roasted tomatoes and rosemary Turkish bread. Great coffees, too.

C

Subiaco

Boucla

349 Rokeby Road; tel: 08-9381 2841; www.boucla.com; Mon–Sat 8am–4pm; train: Subiaco; map p.132 B2

Boucla is a treat. Fight your way past Turkish rugs to the counter, where there are no menus and no price lists. All food is cooked fresh that day, and whatever is on display is what's left.

Brew-Ha

3–4/162 Rokeby Road; tel: 08-9388 7272; www.brewha.com.au; daily 6.30am–6pm; train: Subiaco; map p.132 B3

It may get crazily busy, but that's the beauty of Brew-Ha. The spirited café is a great meeting place and they roast their own coffee on site.

Café Café

Subiaco Square; tel: 08-9388 9800; daily 6.30am–5pm; train: Subiaco; map p.132 B4

Serving some of Perth's best coffee, this café is packed at weekends. They also bake great muffins and have good cooked breakfasts along with cakes, croissants and paninis.

Delizioso

94 Rokeby Road; tel: 08-9381 7796; Mon–Sat 8am–5pm, Thur until 8pm; train: Subiaco; map p.132 B3

The best thing about this little café is its Italian pizza by the slice. Toppings include eggplant and chilli, potato and rosemary, and straight cheese and herbs. On Wednesdays and Thursdays they also sell traditional round pizzas.

Louis Baxters

2/50 Subiaco Square; tel: 08-9380 4203; www.louisbaxters.com.au; Mon–Sat from 7am for breakfast and lunch; train: Subiaco; map p.132 B4

Small and funky, new kid on the block Louis Baxters has quickly become the café of choice among groovy local people and is a warm space featuring commissioned artwork by local artists, and a mix of new and repurposed furniture.

Below: a server at Delizioso brandishes a tray of pizza slices.

Stimulatte

361 Hay Street; tel: 08-9381 1224; Mon–Fri 6.30am–3pm; train: Subiaco; map p.132 B3

Popular with coffee-loving Subiaco-slickers, this buzzing little café serves a selection of healthy lunch options as well as great coffee. Seating is limited.

The Walk Café

5/97 Rokeby Road; tel: 08-9381 2466; www.thewalkcafe.com.au; Mon–Wed 9am–4pm, Thur–Sun 7.30am–4pm; train: Subiaco; map p.132 B2

Just off the main street down Forrest Walk pedestrian mall, this is a 'Subi' favourite. It's always busy yet the service is still great, and the food is delicious and well priced.

Fremantle

Aubergine

231 South Terrace, South Fremantle; tel: 08-9335 2115; daily 6.30am–3pm; train: Fremantle then walk 15 minutes down South Terrace; bus: Fremantle CAT

You'll need to fight for a breakfast table at this local favourite but once seated, Aubergine offers one of the best spots in South Freo for people-watching – the area is home to cool, well-heeled artists, designers and writers, so there's plenty to see.

Benny's Bar and Café

10–12 South Terrace; tel: 08-9433 1333; www.bennys.com.au; daily 7am–late; train: Fremantle

Serves café-style dishes and fusion food, as well as filling Italian. Pop in for oysters, cocktails and live jazz, or settle in for some Freo people-watching on the cappuccino strip.

Flipside Burger Bar

239 Queen Victoria Street, North Fremantle; tel: 08-9433 2188; www.flipsideburgerbar.com.au; Tue–Wed 5.30–9pm, Thur–Fri

noon–2.30pm, 5.30–9pm,
Sat–Sun noon–9pm; train: North
Fremantle

Light and airy burger bar
serving gourmet burgers,
including some of their original creations, such as
chicken, pear and Parme-
san, as well as the classic
beef, egg, bacon, beetroot
and cheese combo. The
menu also caters to vegetar-
ians, with chickpea patties.

Gino's
1 South Terrace; tel: 08-9336
1464; www.ginoscafe.com.au;
daily 7am–10.30pm; train:
Fremantle

Gino's is a fixture on the
Fremantle scene. You will find
families and other local people as well as tourists, all sitting down for a cappuccino
while watching the world go
by. The menu is extensive,
and caters for all tastes with
typical café-style fare. Always
full of life.

Moore & Moore
46 Henry Street; tel: 08-9335
8825; www.mooreandmoore
cafe.com; daily 7am–4pm; train:
Fremantle

This uber-funky café is
located in the Moores Building Contemporary Art Gallery,
one of Perth's most exciting
venues for contemporary art.
Like the gallery, everything in
the café is arty, including its
customers.

Ootong & Lincoln
258 South Terrace, South
Fremantle; tel: 08-9335 6109;
www.ootongandlincoln.com.au;
daily 6.30am–5pm; train:
Fremantle then walk 15 minutes
down South Terrace; bus:
Fremantle CAT

Nostalgic 1950s memora-
bilia decorates the walls at
Ootong & Lincoln, and customers sit at mismatched
furniture while tucking into
one of Freo's best break-
fasts. The lunch is pretty
good too.

Above: several cafés serve heartier mains as well as lighter bites.

Cottesloe, Claremont, Swanbourne and Scarborough

Barchetta
149 Marine Parade, Cottesloe; tel:
08-9385 2411; web n/a; daily
6am–late; bus: 102

If you were any closer to the
water, you'd be in it. Barchetta hangs over the dunes of
North Cottesloe Beach, producing simple dishes with a
European influence. Lunches
include paella and spicy
roast pumpkin salad, and
the dinner menu might
include chermoula lamb and
crab spaghettini.

Barista
38 Napoleon Street, Cottesloe;
tel: 08-9383 3545; web n/a;
daily 6am–10.30pm; bus: 102,
103

Serving simple yet tasty modern Australian food, Barista
makes an effort to keep
healthy options on the menu,
and the food is always fresh.

The Blue Duck
151 Marine Parade, Cottesloe;
tel: 08-9385 2499; daily
6am–late; bus: 102

Overlooking the ocean at
North Cottesloe, this has
been a Perth institution

since 1988. Light breakfasts
start at 6am, with à la carte
from 7am and buffets at the
weekend. From lunch time
it's always busy and you'll
have to book to get a table
overlooking the ocean. The
menu focuses on seafood,
but you'll find many other
options too. If nothing else,
come for coffee and eggs
while enjoying the early
morning light.

Cimbalino
16 Napoleon Street, Cottesloe;
tel: 08-9385 6177; daily
7am–5pm; train: Cottesloe

Grab an espresso at the bar,
or take a seat and enjoy one
of Cimbalino's famous pitta
wraps – either way you'll be
rubbing shoulders with serious coffee connoisseurs
and Cottesloe's glitterati.

> People in Perth take their coffee
> so seriously that baristas often
> refuse (and can get away with
> it) to do anything in a café other
> than make coffee (no table-
> clearing for them), and cooking
> schools and cafés offer classes
> on how to make perfect
> espresso using home machines.

Children

For children, the safe, relaxed environment, relatively small scale and open spaces make Perth perfect for adventures. With several child-oriented attractions and events, keeping the young ones amused is simple. There are also plenty of places where both children and adults can be accommodated; beaches and parks with new play equipment, barbecues and plenty of space, often with a great view, mean that everyone can be happy. If you are in Perth while the school holidays are on, you'll find even more arranged activities that you can tap into by looking in the daily paper, *The West Australian*.

Activities

Extra events and projects are put on at venues during school holidays; details can be obtained from the **Perth Visitor Centre** (tel: 1300-361 351).

Adventure World
179 Progress Drive, Bibra Lake; tel: 08-9417 9666; www.adventureworld.net.au; Oct–Apr: daily 10am–5pm during school holidays, Thur–Mon out of holiday times; admission charge; train: Cockburn, then bus: 520 to Gwilliam Drive
There's unlimited use of all the rides and attractions once you have paid the quite high entry fee to enter this big adventure park. 'The Big Kahuna' is the park's largest and newest ride with over 1,000 sq m/yds of water-based fun. There are also giant swings, water slides, water tubing, ghost tunnels, a roller-coaster and lots more. The kids will love it – mum and dad will probably go home with a headache.

Aquarium of Western Australia (AQWA)
Hillary's Boat Harbour; tel: 08-9447 7500; www.aqwa.com.au; daily 10am–5pm; admission charge; train: Clarkson, then bus: 456

AQWA is a wonderful place for children. Western Australia has 12,000km (7,400 miles) of coastline, and five distinct coastal environments are recreated here. The highlight, however, is the walk-through aquarium representing the 'Shipwreck Coast', where sharks, loggerhead turtles, stingrays and more glide smoothly overhead within inches of the upturned faces watching them. Other highlights include a touch pool, saltwater crocodiles of the far north coast and tropical fish of the Coral Coast. The aquarium also offers the opportunity to dive and snorkel with sharks.

Awesome Festival
Various locations; tel: 08-9485 0560; www.awesomearts.com
Each November the Awesome International Arts Festival for Bright Young Things encourages young people and their adult friends to experience an extraordinary array of both free and ticketed film, animation, music, sculpture, installation and new media in the Perth

Below: a friendly dolphin at AQWA.

Left: the Awesome Festival features exhibits that intrigue all ages; here, a child gets up close to the project, *Guixot De 8*, a conversion of scrap metals into interactive installations.

Kings Park

Off Kings Park Road; tel: 08-9480 3600; www.bgpa.wa.gov.au; park daily 24 hours, Park Visitor Information daily 9.30am–4pm; free; bus: 102, 78, 24, 37; map p.133 D2

The Lotterywest Family Area is a recently refurbished playground designed specifically for families with young children. It has two playgrounds, one designed for children under the age of five, leafy parkland with plenty of barbecues and the popular Stickybeaks Café. In another section of the park you can take a walk across the Federation Walkway, which is actually a curved glass-and-metal walk through the tree tops, looking over the Swan River.
SEE ALSO PARKS, P.89

Maritime Museum

Victoria Quay, Fremantle; tel: 08-9431 8444; www.museum.wa.gov.au/maritime; daily 9.30am–5pm; admission charge; train: Fremantle

The spectacular building that

Perth has its own free parents' newspaper. While not exactly an essay on beautiful design, it is functional and packed with info. You'll find it free at a range of locations, in particular newsagents and delis. If you are staying somewhere swish, ask reception nicely and they might be able to track one down for you. See www.kidsinperth.com.

CBD. Installations have included Ixilum, a giant inflatable walk-through experience, where people are invited to wander through the various inflated 'rooms', each made from different coloured fabric.
SEE ALSO FESTIVALS AND EVENTS, P.55

Caversham Wildlife Park

Within Whiteman Park; tel: 08-9248 1984; www.caversham wildlife.com.au; daily 9am–5.30pm; admission charge; best by car, by train: Bassendean, then bus 955 or 956 to Whiteman Park

Caversham is home to West-ern Australia's largest collection of native animals. Feed the kangaroos, meet koalas and wombats and watch interactive farm shows featuring sheep-shearing, sheep dogs working, stockmen on horses, billy tea-making, whip-cracking, bottle-feeding baby lambs and cow milking. The show runs for around an hour. All attractions are included in the entry fee. Caversham is in the grounds of Whiteman Park *(see p.39)*.

Right: exploring the Maritime Museum.

If getting around the city on foot doesn't appeal to tired little ones, jump aboard Sightseeing Perth's double decker 'Hop On Hop Off' bus. A two-day pass allows you to hop on and off as you please and takes you past city highlights including Kings Park and Botanic Gardens, Northbridge, Crown Perth, the WACA, Perth Mint; the Museum & Art Gallery of WA, shopping malls and much more. A family pass for two adults and two children is $55, and this includes discounts to Perth's major tourist attractions. Barrack Street Jetty and 565 Hay Street (between Pier and Barrack) are just two of the 13 stops where you can jump on. Tickets are available on board (tel: 08-9203 8882; www.citysight seeingperth.com).

houses the Maritime Museum was opened in 2003 and contains six themed areas: naval defence, the Indian Ocean, Fremantle and the Swan River, Hooked on Fishing, Cargoes and Tin Canoe to the America's Cup-Winning *Australia II*. *Australia II* is suspended at one end of the museum, and there are lots of quirky delights to discover. SEE ALSO MUSEUMS AND GALLERIES, P.78

Perth Zoo
20 Labouchere Road, South Perth; tel: 08-9474 3551; www.perthzoo.wa.gov.au; daily 9am–5pm; admission charge; bus: 30, 31; ferry from Barrack Street to Mends Street; map p.138 A2
The Perth Zoo is great fun to explore, with 1,800 animals and 120 staff. There has been a focus over the years on creating habitats for animals that mimic their natural homes, so you will find an

African Savannah area complete with red dirt, rhinos and giraffes; an Asian rainforest, home to Asian elephants, and Sumatran tigers and orangutans; and an Australian Bushwalk through recreations of different Australian ecosystems. There is a small train that can take you around the grounds, plus throughout the day you can visit various enclosures to listen to the zookeepers talk about their charges. The grounds are also lovely; you can easily spend a leisurely day here. Download the free interactive Perth Zoo iPhone app from the website.

Scitech
City West, Sutherland Street; tel: 08-9215 0700; Mon–Fri 9.30am–4pm, Sat–Sun and school holidays 10am–5pm; admission charge; train: City West; map p.133 E4
A science discovery centre with fascinating hands-on experiments and child-

oriented (sometimes icky, to an adult mind) special topics. Kids get to discover many aspects of science, including light, electricity, sound, and much more.

It is all delivered in a creative, fun and very interactive way. Puppet shows are aimed at three- to seven-year-olds, and there's a theatre performance on varying topics. Entry price includes Horizon – the Planetarium, a stadium-like indoor theatre presenting high-tech shows with a focus on science and space.

Western Australian Museum
Perth Cultural Centre, James Street; tel: 08-9212 3700; www.museum.wa.gov.au/ oursites/perth/perth.asp; daily 9.30am–5pm; free; train: Perth; map p.134 B3
Apart from being a genuinely interesting visit at any time of the year, the museum organises special

Below: having fun with a street performer in Subiaco.

children's activities during school holidays. There is a large hall featuring an array of stuffed animals, including a very large bison. Kids won't want to miss the dinosaurs, either. There is also a spectacular butterfly display which shows the beauty and colour of the insects. There is a dedicated area for children, too.
SEE ALSO MUSEUMS AND GALLERIES, P.77

Whiteman Park

Lord Street, Whiteman; tel: 08-9209 6000; www.caversham wildlife.com.au; daily 8.30am–5.30pm; free; best by car, or train: Bassendean, then bus: 955 or 956 to Whiteman Park.
Only 30 minutes' drive from central Perth, this 4,050-hectare (10,000-acre) park is a great place for children. A variety of steam and diesel locomotives can take you around the park, or there's an electric tram to a picnic area. Bike hire, a children's pool, an unreal playground and mini electric cars are among the other attractions.

Essentials

For essentials such as nappies, baby formula and other small child essentials, any supermarket will be able to help. The large supermarkets are **Coles** and **Woolworths**, and these are found throughout the suburbs, shopping centres and the city. There are also local supermarkets, often with longer trading hours, which can supply these items, along with basic medical needs such as headache medication, band aids, antiseptic cream and so on.

There are many late-night chemists around Perth who can also supply all these things, although you will pay more for them. There will

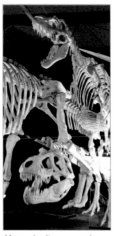

Above: the dinosaurs at the Western Australian Museum.

always be a pharmacist on duty who can give advice on over-the-counter medication if your child is ill. Two central late-night chemists are:

Beaufort Street 24 Hour Chemist

647 Beaufort Street, Mount Lawley; tel: 08-9328 7775; daily 24 hours; bus: 67, 60, 21

Stirling Drive In Pharmacy

234 Stirling Highway, Claremont; tel: 08-9384 2292; daily 8am–11pm; bus: 102, 103
If you need to try to get to

one of the late-night chemists late at night, you will be better off calling a taxi, as the wait for public transport at night can be lengthy.

If you need a doctor, either look in the **Yellow Pages** (there will be a yellow directory book where you are staying) or call Health Direct 24-hour advice line (toll-free: 1800-022 222). You can also find hospital information in the front pages of the **White Pages** (residential and business phone listings). If you need an ambulance, police or fire department, call 000 only in an emergency. Emergency hospitals include Perth's children's hospital:

Princess Margaret Hospital

Roberts Road, Subiaco; tel: 08-9340 8222; www.pmh.health.wa.gov.au
Two other top city hospitals are:

Royal Perth Hospital

Wellington Street; tel: 08-9224 2244 (emergency); www.rph.wa.gov.au

Sir Charles Gairdiner Hospital

Hospital Avenue, Nedlands; tel: 08-9346 3333; www.scgh.health.wa.gov.au

Below: cycling in Kings Park.

Environment

Australia has one of the most variable rainfall patterns in the world. While the east coast has been battered with flooding and cyclones, Perth remains in drought. Water restrictions have been in place for a number of years: households are only permitted to use sprinklers two days a week, and it is recommended that they only stay on for 10–15 minutes. Perth is currently saving more water than has been targeted, and in other environmental matters is in a decent state. Energy-saving measures are encouraged, the air is clean, as are the waterways, and only on rare occasions does smog build up over the city.

Green Measures

Kings Park *(see Parks, p.89)* helps Perth to keep clean, with the large area of vegetation effectively cleaning much of the city's air. Perth is also one of the windiest cities on earth, and the strong breezes that come in each day from the Indian Ocean effectively blow any pollution away from the city.

The global push for businesses and individuals to consider their carbon footprint hasn't passed Perth by, either. You'll see many cars driving around with stickers proclaiming that they are carbon-neutral (a popular site, run by **Men of the Trees**, is www.carbon neutral.com.au, a calculator that allows you to add up your entire carbon output and 'neutralise' it by paying them to plant trees) and all state government vehicles are now carbon-neutral as well. Many businesses have also taken similar steps in paying external operators to ensure that their business and employees are carbon-

neutral, with some using it as a marketing opportunity.

Perth has also participated in the global movement called Earth Hour, where people are encouraged to turn off all their electricity for an hour on a Saturday night. Bigger cities in Australia have shown more public support, but the interest has been proven to be there.

The City of Perth is also doing its best to keep the CBD as clean and green as possible. It is partnered with city councils throughout Aus-

Below: the Serpentine Dam, just outside Perth, at one of the city's main water supplies.

Native Flora and Fauna

The spectacular wild flowers scattered across Western Australia's vast landscape mean spring is fondly referred to as WA's 'snow season'. Western Australia's broad climatic range sees more than 12,000 wild-flower species colour the state for about five months of the year – one of Australia's longest wild-flower seasons. Much of this, however, is not seen in the city area; you'll need to head north towards Kalbarri, or south towards Esperance, to see the carpets of spring everlastings and delicate orchids.

The best city place to view native flora is in Kings Park, especially during spring, where native kangaroo paws and everlastings dominate the park's scenery.

Western Australia is one of the world's most bio-diverse areas, with new species being discovered regularly, which is unheard of in other parts of the world. You are most likely to see the most famous of Australia's creatures in wildlife parks, like Caversham Wildlife Park, but you may be lucky and catch a glimpse if you head out to the country surrounding Perth.

SEE ALSO CHILDREN, P.37

tralia to join the national CitySwitch Green Office Programme, an initiative that works with office tenants to achieve improved energy efficiency, thereby reducing CO_2 emissions.

Recycling is popular among Perth households, with each council in charge of how they run their programme. Large recycling bins are also available in some public spaces, such as beaches with food facilities. There is usually a bin for glass, for plastic, for paper and for general rubbish.

Water Restrictions

Due to the years of drought and Perth's dry climate, homeowners are changing their gardening styles. With continuing restrictions on watering gardens, drought-tolerant plants and native species are more popular than before, and water-saving soil additives are often used, too.

A heavy advertising campaign has educated local people to be thoughtful about their water consumption. The dam levels are still very low (under 40 percent full), and have gone as low as 17 percent since 2002.

The WA government has been much slower to act than other states, and perhaps the continuing low dam levels are an example of this. Other major Australian cities have also introduced a ban on washing cars at home (drivers have to take their cars to a car wash, which now all use recycled water); however, Perth has not yet taken this measure.

A Clean City

Public littering is frowned upon in Perth. There are lots of public bins available, and local people are very proud of their clean environment. There are fines for littering, and even something as small as a cigarette butt is considered offensive, as cigarette butts are known to end up in the ocean and river, and can plug the breathing hole of dolphins. You can often see dolphins in the Swan River, which brings home the immediate threat to them.

When visiting many of Perth's beaches you'll have to walk through a dune area. There are marked paths which you should stick to, not just for safety in avoiding snakes, but also because these areas are very sensitive and often are undergoing re-vegetation. Native plants, no matter how plain they might appear, are protected in WA.

Essentials

These listings cover the sensible details that you'll need for your journey. A trip to Western Australia should be simple and relatively carefree, especially if you are aware of a few basics, such as how to keep safe and healthy (including avoiding nasty sunburn), when shops and banks open, how to make a call or post a letter and what to pack. Perthites are friendly folk and generally happy to provide assistance if you aren't sure about something or need directions. If in doubt, ask at your hotel or pay a visit to the tourist office. Note that further practical details can be found in *Children, p.39,* and *Transport, p.118–21.*

Budgeting for Your trip

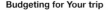

While Perth's economy is still strong, despite the global economic crisis, this generally is not reflected in visitors' costs. In general, these compare favourably with the UK and are probably on a par with the US. Public transport is very cheap (free CAT buses in Perth city centre, for example), and petrol is considerably cheaper than in the UK.

Admission charges to sights and attractions are fairly low, and often free at museums. Concession rates are available in many places on production of a valid senior or student card.

Climate

TEMPERATURES

Average temperatures are: winter: 18°C (65°F), spring: 22°C (72°F), summer: 32°C (86°F), autumn: 24°C (75°F). If these temperatures sound high, remember that WA's low humidity makes them more bearable.

WEATHER

Perth's Mediterranean-style climate means that the sun shines most days, all year. Most of the year's rain falls during the winter months (June–Aug), easing off in spring (Sept–Nov). The city is often dry for months on end, and summer (Dec–Feb) can be very hot, with temperatures often reaching the high 30s Celsius (95–102°F).

WHAT TO PACK

Lightweight clothing is best most of the year, a few layers, plus cool, comfortable shoes or sandals. Even in winter one good sweater, a lightweight jacket and scarf will be sufficient, plus an umbrella. Coats are rarely seen in Perth. Informality is the general rule, and you'll be comfortable in casual clothes just about everywhere, with the exception of better

Electricity is rated at 230–50 volts, 50 hertz. Standard plugs have three flat pins, and you may need an adaptor for heavier-use appliances such as hairdryers. Universal outlets for 110 volts (for shavers, etc.) are found in most accommodation.

restaurants and places such as the theatre. Hats, sunglasses and sunblock are strongly advised, as the sun is fierce during the summer.

Crime and Safety

EMERGENCIES

Fire, police or ambulance emergency services: dial 000. **Non-emergency police attendance:** dial 131 444.

ON THE BEACH

Parked cars, especially those emblazoned with hire-company stickers, are a target for petty thieves. If possible, leave nothing in the car; your belongings are safer with you on the sand.

Beach safety extends to the ocean, too. Swim only where there are lifeguards, or the water is very placid. Take extra care on rocks where waves are pounding; occasionally, freak waves have washed people away.

SECURITY

Perth is a relatively safe place, with no unusual risks or problems, but in any big city a certain level of care

Left: evening rush hour in Perth.

sible public transport and parking, toilets, and easy access routes through the city.

PUBLIC TRANSPORT
Central Area Transit (CAT) buses provide a free, frequent and wheelchair-accessible bus service.

Railway staff are available to assist wheelchair users to access metro trains. Wheelchairs and motorised scooters can be hired from: Citiplace Community Centre, Perth Railway Station upper level; tel: 08-9325 3264; Mon–Fri 8.30am–3.45pm. A deposit of A$20 and proof of identification are needed; bookings are advisable. Reciprocal ACROD parking rights apply to overseas visitors for up to three months.

Embassies and Consulates
British Consular Agency Level 26, Allendale Square, 77 St Georges Terrace; tel: 08-9224 4700.
Canadian Consulate 267 St Georges Terrace; tel: 08-9322 7930.
US Consulate General 16 St Georges Terrace; tel: 08-9202 1224.

Below: one of many internet cafés in Perth.

must be taken. Be extra vigilant late at night, especially in the vicinity of bars and clubs. At this time a taxi is probably the best way to move around, unless you're just walking a short way on busier, well-lit streets. Lock car doors and don't leave valuables or bags on display in parked cars.

WILDLIFE
Be vigilant when walking in the bush, wetlands, or around lakes and rivers, near sand dunes and on Rottnest Island. Stay on paths, or where you have a clear view ahead. Snakes are the only dangerous animals you might encounter. They want to avoid you as much as you do them, and most snakes will move away when they feel the vibrations of your footfall.

Customs
Fruits and vegetables must not be brought into Australia, and any other food you're carrying must be declared. The regulations are prominently displayed on arrival, and failure to comply can result in very large penalties.

Duty free allowance is: A$900 worth of goods (not including tobacco or alcohol, and reduced to A$450 for under 18s); 2.25l of alcohol in total, including wine, beer and spirits; 250 cigarettes, or 250g of tobacco/cigars.

Under a Tourist Refund Scheme the GST (General Sales Tax) on goods bought in Australia can be refunded on departure at the airport. This applies only to goods carried as hand luggage, or worn to travel; value must be a minimum of A$300, spent in one store, shown on a single invoice; goods must be bought within 30 days of departure. To claim the tax refund, wear or carry the goods to the Tourist Refund Scheme office (beyond customs and immigration desks), together with the invoice, your passport and boarding pass.

Disabled Travellers
The starting point for disabled travellers should be the city's website: www.perth.wa.gov.au.

Access maps show how to get around and feature acces-

Above: ATMs are scattered around the city.

Entry Requirements

Passports are required by all nationalities. Visas are also necessary for all but visitors from New Zealand. No vaccinations are required.

Health and Medical Care

If a medical problem arises while in Australia, phone the **Health Direct** 24-hour advice line: toll-free: 1800-022 2220.

BUYING MEDICINES

Pharmacies dispense prescribed medication. They also sell non-prescription medication, plus toiletries, cosmetics and film, and can often advise on minor problems. Check **Yellow Pages** for the most conveniently located pharmacies and for listings of those that are open late.
SEE ALSO CHILDREN, P.39

DENTISTS

Many dentists practise in or near the city centre. Find the most convenient surgery or those with late hours in **Yellow Pages**; or call any hospital A&E department.
Lifecare Dental (Perth)
419 Wellington Street (Forrest Chase, opposite the train station); tel: 08-9221 2777; daily

Perth and the rest of Western Australia is eight hours in advance of GMT.

8am–8pm
They take emergency cases.

INSURANCE

British citizens are covered by a reciprocal agreement with Australia, which usually covers emergency health care only, not pre-existing medical conditions. Reciprocal agreements are also in place with Finland, Italy, Malta, Netherlands, New Zealand and Sweden. Passport-holders from these countries can reclaim the cost of treatment from Medicare in Australia. As most travellers will not qualify for free treatment, it's wise to take out health insurance. The basic cost of consulting a doctor is A$65.

MOSQUITOES

Use insect repellent, especially around still water, at dusk and in the early morning. Some mosquitoes carry viruses, so try to avoid being bitten.

SUNBURN

The Australian sun is very harsh. Hats and sunglasses are essential most of the year. You will burn quickly if you don't take precautions. On the water, the reflection will make you burn even if you are under cover. Always wear sunscreen and cover up as much as possible.

Internet

There are numerous internet cafés in Perth, especially in the Barrack Street and William Street area, and most hotels and backpacker hostels have access.
Britannia on William Backpackers
253 William Street Northbridge; tel: 08-9227 6000.
Internet Station
131 William Street; tel: 08-9226 5373.

Money

ATM MACHINES

These are common in the city but far less so in rural areas, although you will often find an ATM in a pub or petrol station if there are no banks in town. Your ATM card will need to be part of the Plus or Cirrus network.

CREDIT CARDS

Credit cards, especially Visa, are widely accepted. Some places charge service fees.

CURRENCY

The Australian dollar (A$) is the local currency. Coin denominations are 5, 10, 20 and 50 cents, and A$1 and A$2. Notes come in denominations of A$5, A$10, A$20, A$50 and A$100.

FOREIGN EXCHANGE

Banks are generally the best places to change currency. Some hotels will exchange major currencies for guests, and there is a 24-hour agency at the airport.

TAXES

A General Sales Tax (GST) of 10 percent applies to most purchases. Departure tax is included in the ticket price.

TRAVELLER'S CHEQUES

International traveller's cheques will be cashed at

airports, banks, hotels and motels. **Travelex** (tel: 08-9322 6277) has several city branches; the major one is in Murray Street Mall (Mon–Fri 9am–5pm, Sat 10am–1pm, Sun 12noon–4pm). Fees and rates vary. The **WA Tourist Centre** (see right) will exchange major traveller's cheques and currency. It is advisable to change your money before heading out of Perth or Fremantle, as banks are rare in the countryside.

Opening Hours

Shopping hours are generally: Mon–Thur 9am–5.30pm, Fri 9am–9pm, Sat 9am–5pm, Sun 11am–5pm. Sunday opening is confined to central Perth, Fremantle and Rockingham. Suburban shops trade until 9pm on Thursday, rather than Friday nights. Banking hours are: Mon–Thur 9.30am–4pm, Fri 9.30am–5pm. Most banks are closed on Saturdays.

Postal Services

Post offices are open 9am–5pm, Mon–Fri, and the central post office in Forrest Chase also opens Saturday morning, 9am–12.30pm and Sunday, noon–4pm. See www.auspost.com.au.

Smoking

In 2006, WA banned smoking in all enclosed public places, with the exception of the International Room at **Burswood Casino**. The Healthway Quit campaign has resulted in open-air sports stadiums banning smoking. If you are in doubt as to where a venue's designated smoking areas are, ask staff or look for the signs.

Telephones

MOBILE PHONES
The best course of action is to buy a 'phone card' (actu-ally simply a receipt with a PIN number that you insert in front of the number you wish to dial), which you can use with your own mobile phone and can also be used in public phone boxes. There are some very inexpensive deals around: ask the vendor for advice. TravelSIM cards are available from most post offices and also offer travellers cheap rates (www.travelsim.net.au).

PUBLIC PHONES
Local calls from public phones cost 50¢. Long-distance calls to Australian and overseas numbers can be made from most phones, including public phones and hotels. Some public phones operate by card, available from post offices and large newsagents. For up-to-date rates and information, make a toll-free call to **Telstra** (tel: 13 22 00).

For overseas calls, dial 0011, followed by the country code and number.

Tipping

Tipping is not obligatory and not expected, but if you have had especially good service and wish to tip, you will not offend. Likewise, it is not necessary to tip taxi drivers, but it is usual to round up the fare to the nearest dollar or two.

Tourist Office

Western Australia Tourist Centre

Corner of Wellington Street and Forrest Place; tel: 1300-361 351; www.wavisitorcentre.com; May–Aug: Mon–Thur 8.30am–5.30pm, Fri 8.30am–6pm, Sat 9.30am–4.30pm, Sun noon–4.30pm, Sept–Apr: Mon–Thur 8.30am–6pm, Fri 8.30am–7pm, Sat 9.30am–4.30pm, Sun noon–4.30pm; train: Perth; map p.134 A2

Located across the road from the central Perth train station, this visitor centre has a large range of touring options, and will also book these tours for you. There is also a wide range of accommodation, transport, maps and other brochures to help with your stay.

Below: the Western Australian flag.

Excursions

Perth is an attractive city, but in order to appreciate fully the natural variety and beauty of this part of Australia, you need to venture a little further afield. In this most remote corner of Australia, local people think nothing of driving for three hours or longer to reach places that they consider close to the city. Visitors can choose to self-drive or to join an organised tour. Alternatively, bus services operate daily to many destinations (call the Transwa information line, tel: 1300-662 205, or visit www.transwa.wa.gov.au for timetables). The roads are good, the traffic is easy, and you would have to try very hard to get lost.

West of Perth

ROTTNEST ISLAND

Rottnest Island Authority; tel: 08-9432 9111; www.rottnest island.com
Rottnest Express, C Shed, Fremantle; tel: 08-9335 6406; Barrack Street, Perth; tel: 08-9421 5888
Oceanic Cruises; tel: 08-9325 1191

19km (12 miles) from Fremantle

Rotto, as the locals affectionately call Rottnest Island, is a 30-minute ferry ride from Fremantle, yet feels as though it is a world away. In its chequered history it has gone through many incarnations, including as a penal settlement and a military occupied zone, before emerging as the holiday island it is known as today. It is loved by local people who escape to the island to laze on picture-postcard beaches, snorkel in azure waters and dive among the shipwrecks that litter its coastline. Strict environmental policies keep the developers out and the traffic to a bare minimum, helping to preserve the island's sense of timelessness for future generations to enjoy.

The island is about 11km (7 miles) long and 4.5km (3 miles) at its widest. Facilities on the island are relatively basic, but have improved in recent years. Hotel accommodation is limited to the **Rottnest Lodge** and the recently renovated **Hotel**

Below: a game-fishing boat *(left)* and the Basin Beach *(right)* at Rottnest Island.

Left: the dramatic Pinnacles at sunset.

There are limited options for travelling by rail when making these excursions; unless you join up with a tour group (details throughout this chapter), self-driving is your best option, but remember to keep good supplies of water in your car if driving on a hot day. Details of car hire companies can be found in *Transport, p.121.*

Rottnest. Formerly the Quokka Arms, the hotel now offers comfortable accommodation, a slick, modern 'beer garden' and a bistro-style restaurant. Upgraded self-contained cottages and villas are also popular accommodation choices. At peak times, accommodation is allocated by public ballot, as demand is so high. If you want to stay overnight or longer, make sure you book well in advance. All bookings, including tours, are best done through the Rottnest Island Authority website *(see left)*.

Nothing sums up the pace of life on Rottnest more than the humble two-wheeler, the time-honoured form of transport on the island. With virtually no traffic on the roads, cycling is a real pleasure here, and the stunning views certainly make all the hills worth the effort. Allow about 2½ hours to make the 24km (15-mile) round trip. You can either bring your own bike (they are carried free on the ferries) or hire one through the Rottnest Island Authority

or Rottnest Express when you book your ferry ticket. Note that by law you must wear a helmet when riding a bike anywhere in WA.

If that seems like too much hard work, the Bayseeker bus is a hop-on, hop-off service that loops between all the best beaches and the main settlement at Thomson Bay. It is designed to carry everything from surfboards to fishing rods, so it is the ideal way to get around. A day pass is very reasonable (tickets available from the Visitor Centre, *see below*). The trip from Geordie Bay to the Thomson Bay settlement is free, and a courtesy shuttle bus also plies this route.

Directly opposite the end of the jetty is the **Visitor and Information Centre** (tel: 08-9372 9732), an excellent resource for planning all aspects of your visit to Rottnest. Behind the Visitor Centre is a pedestrian shopping mall with a general store, post office, newsagent, cafés, a chemist and fashion boutique.

The **Basin** is generally regarded as the best swimming beach, only 10 minutes from Thomson Bay. Other sheltered spots include **Longreach Bay**, **Little Parakeet Bay** and **Little Salmon Bay**. **Geordie Bay** has new holiday accommodation, shops and a picturesque bay filled with bobbing boats.

Rottnest is home to some remarkable species of coral and fish, and its crystal waters create optimum snorkelling and diving conditions. Experienced divers may want to join a trip out to one of the many wrecks lying offshore, which are havens for all kinds of sea creatures. **Charter 1** runs guided snorkel and dive tours from the island and Rottnest Island Bike Hire offers dive tank refills (tel: 08-9292 5105). Snorkellers can pick up an underwater trail at Parker Point – a stunning beach where the crystal-clear turquoise waters offer excellent visibility. The Visitor Centre can provide maps, gear hire, bookings and pointers on the best reefs to visit.

Another nice way of exploring the island is on foot. Walking tours, run by knowledgeable volunteer guides,

47

depart daily from the Visitor Centre. They cover a range of subjects, from Aboriginal history on the island to environmental issues. Most are free; some make a small charge.
SEE ALSO ABORIGINAL CULTURE, P.26–7

North of Perth

LANCELIN AND THE PINNACLES
127km (80 miles) from Perth;
www.lancelin.org.au
The coastal area stretching north from Lancelin to Kalbarri is known for its perfect beaches, met by rugged gorges and wildflower plains. This area is excellent for fishing, windsurfing and snorkelling, and even facilitates activities such as sand-boarding. The coastal town of Lancelin is protected by two large rock islands and surrounded by towering sand dunes. It is reached easily from Perth by heading north along Wanneroo Road, which becomes Lancelin Road.

For a real adrenalin rush, you may want to give sand-boarding a go. **Go West Tours** (tel: 08-9791 3818) runs day tours from Perth that include sand-boarding, exploration of the Nambung

National Park and a walk through the Pinnacles.

From Lancelin, one of the most popular excursions is to the eerie **Pinnacles Desert**, in the heart of the **Nambung National Park**, about 245km (152 miles) north of Perth. Considered one of WA's most distinctive attractions, the Pinnacles Desert is an extensive area of stone monuments that rise up from the desert floor, some reaching up to 3m (15ft) high. Most major coach tours include a stop at the Pinnacles on their northbound itineraries. If you are self-driving, take Nambung National Park Pinnacles Drive off the Brand Highway. From the car park (admission charge A$10 per vehicle), it's a short walk to the Pinnacles area, although if weather conditions are poor, a 4WD might be necessary to enter the park. A circular track leads around the park, with a lookout at the northern end.

NEW NORCIA
132km (82 miles) from Perth;
www.newnorcia.wa.edu.au
An easy and popular excur-

sion from Perth (often combined with a trip to the Pinnacles) is to the Benedictine community of New Norcia, situated in the middle of the bush, a two-hour journey by car along the Great Northern Highway.

WA's only monastic town, comprising 64 buildings laid out in a cross formation, New Norcia was founded by Dom Rosendo Salvado, a missionary, in 1846. Visitors who want to explore at their own pace can take the **New Norcia Heritage Trail**, an easy 2km (1¼-mile) walk linking most of the major sites (details can be found at the Museum and Art Gallery, below). Alternatively, a two-hour guided walking tour departs daily from the **Museum and Art Gallery** entrance at 11am and 1.30pm (tel: 08-9654 8056). This includes entrance to the monks' private chapel, and concludes with the opportunity to sample tasty treats from the New Norcia bakery,

If you're heading east out of Perth along Toodyay Road, you'll soon reach Toodyay, a pretty, historic town that's perfect for an easy day trip. The Prospector, the train that travels between the East Perth Terminal and Kalgoorlie, also stops in town, making rail travel to Toodyay a relaxing alternative (www.transwa.wa.gov.au).

such as New Norcia nut cake and Dom Salvado Pan Chocolatti. These New Norcia products are super-tasty and widely available in Perth if you don't make the trek out to the community.

East of Perth

YORK
97km (60 miles) from Perth;
www.yorkwa.com.au
Head east from Perth and within an hour you'll find yourself in Western Australia's lush Avon Valley, home of the historic town of York and kilometre after kilometre of farming country.

Self-driving is an excellent option if you are heading to

Above: Busselton Jetty.

destinations close to the city, such as Toodyay (see box, left). Another historic town is York, 35km (22 miles) south of Northam along Northam Road (from Perth, York is best accessed by taking Great Eastern Highway, then turning right onto Great Southern Highway, which leads directly into town). This tiny town is easy to explore on foot: many of the most impressive buildings and authentic antique stores are located on Avon Terrace, the main street.

South of Perth

Head south of Perth for the region's top wineries, gourmet produce (cheese, chocolate and olive oil), and dense, luscious karri and jarrah forests.

If you're catching the bus from Perth, **Transwa** has a daily service that stops at all major towns on the South Western and Bussell highways (tel: 1300 662205). **South West Coach Lines** also runs a regular service between Perth and the major southwestern towns of Bunbury and Busselton (tel: 08-9753 7700).

BUNBURY
180km (111 miles) from Perth;
www.australiassouthwest.com
From Dwellingup, it's a 1½-

hour drive to the southern city of Bunbury, WA's third-largest population centre. If you're driving, head south on the Kwinana Freeway, which turns into the Forrest Highway leading straight to Bunbury.

One of the main attractions at Bunbury is the **Dolphin Discovery Centre** (Koombana Beach, Koombana Drive; tel: 08-9791 3088; winter: daily 9am–3pm, summer: daily 8am–4pm; admission charge). A community of bottlenose dolphins visits the beach daily to feed, and visitors can stand on the beach within arm's reach of the mammals. Dolphin cruises depart daily in summer, and the centre offers popular 'Swim with the Dolphins' tours. A new 360-degree theatre gives guests up-close insights into the dolphins' habits and habitat.

BUSSELTON
232km (144 miles) from Perth;
www.geographebay.com
The gateway to the **Margaret River Wine Region** (see Wine Country, p.126), Busselton is one of the top destinations for locals and visitors alike. Its location on Geographe Bay, one of only two north-facing, and therefore protected, bays in WA, also makes it perfect for

49

Above: a sample of Western Australia's stunning coastline and the lighthouse at Cape Naturaliste.

families and swimmers. From Bunbury, Busselton is an easy half-hour's drive south along Bussell Highway (if you're coming from Perth, take the South Western Highway south to Busselton).

One of Busselton's most photographed features is **Busselton Jetty**. At over 1,800m (5,900ft) in length, this is the longest wooden pier in the southern hemisphere. It is packed with a range of family-friendly attractions.

The jetty's **Underwater Observatory** (tel: 08-9754 0900; www.busseltonjetty. com.au; daily Sept–Apr: 9am–5pm, May–Aug: 10am–4pm; admission charge) allows visitors to descend 8m (26ft) below sea level for amazing views of vividly coloured corals, sponges, fish and invertebrates. Admission charges include a return train journey, a 40-minute guided tour and all-day jetty access.

The boatshed-style **Interpretive Centre** (summer: 8.30am–6pm, winter: 9am–5pm; admission charge), 50m (165ft) offshore, relates the history of the jetty. You can also watch the underwater world beneath

the jetty via a marine cam, browse through the arts and crafts on display and purchase tickets for the Red Jetty Train that ferries passenger up and down the pier.

DUNSBOROUGH AND YALLINGUP

255km (158 miles) from Perth; www.australiassouthwest.com/ en/Margaret+River+Wine+ Region/Dunsborough/default.htm; www.westernaustralia.com
Dunsborough has excellent beaches, perfect for families. For more secluded beaches follow Naturalist Road, north-east of Dunsborough, to Meelup, Eagle Bay and Bunker Bay. Smith's Beach, off Caves Road and Canal Rocks Road south of Yallingup, is one of the area's best spots for surfing.

Naturaliste Road will also take you to the tip of **Cape Naturaliste** with its old light-house (Tue–Sun 9.30am–4pm; admission charge), built in 1903, and hiking trails. The 135km (84-mile) **Cape to Cape Walk** leads from here to the Cape Leeuwin Lighthouse. It is not as developed as the Bibbul-

mun Track, but winds through the **Leeuwin-Naturaliste National Park**, passing many natural attractions, such as Sugarloaf Rock and Three Bears, the area's best surf break. A guide to the trail is available from the Margaret River Visitor Centre.
SEE ALSO PARKS, P.94

MANDURAH

74km (46 miles) from Perth
From Safety Bay, Highway 1 is the best route to Mandurah, the fastest-growing city in Australia (fast trains also link Mandurah and Perth, making the journey around an hour). Mandurah has a permanent holiday atmosphere, partly because so much of the city overlooks canals, the ocean or the Peel Inlet. Many

Right: the stunning Kalbarri National Park.

Right: Ngilgi Cave, at Yallingup.

of its restaurants, craft shops, art galleries and cultural buildings are set around Mandjar Bay, a lovely location for dining.

Inexpensive estuary and canal cruises are an excellent way to get the feel of this watery city. Several operators can be found on the jetty close to **Mandurah Art Centre**. Skippers are skilled at finding the dolphins that live in the estuary; just to see them surf and barrel-roll ahead of your cruiser is worth the fare.

Fishing is also popular, especially crabbing. On summer weekends, thousands hunt for the local blue mannas, wading the shallows with scoop nets and stout shoes, while others drop crab pots from their boats. The Mandurah crab festival, held in March, is a major annual event.

Dolphin Quay at the new Mandurah Ocean Marina is the place for fish and chips on the boardwalk, markets, canal cruise departures and swanky new accommodation.

MARGARET RIVER
279km (173 miles) from Perth
From Dunsborough and Yallingup, continue south along Caves Road, turning

left at Carters Road to Margaret River. Alternatively, if you are driving from Perth, take the Busselton Bypass and head south to Margaret River on the Bussell Highway.

Margaret River is home to some of WA's top wineries, many of which also have excellent restaurants, which all in all make for very pleasant pit stops. Begin a wine tour at the **Margaret River Regional Wine Centre**, in the **Margaret River Visitor Centre** on Bussell Highway in the heart of town. It holds regular free varietal wine-tastings and can supply maps to all the wineries in the area. If you are not staying overnight, remember to designate a driver for the journey back.
SEE ALSO WINE COUNTRY, P.126–7

If you feel like continuing further afield, take the 591km (366-mile) drive up to **Kalbarri**. Other than flying, driving is the fastest way to get there, rather than taking a bus. However, **Greyhounds Australia** (www.greyhounds.com.au) and **Transwa** (www.transwa.wa. gov.au) operate direct bus services between Perth and Kalbarri. Once in Kalbarri, you can rent a vehicle from **Kalbarri Cars 4U2 Hire** (tel: 08-9937 1290) or **Kalbarri Auto Rentals** (tel: 0409-225 271). Kalbarri has long been a favourite holiday destination for West Australians, with Perthites regularly making the six-hour drive, equipped with snorkel, fishing, surfing and windsurfing gear for the outdoor opportunities on offer. However, the summer months can be scorching in Kalbarri, so for a milder experience, visit the area during winter. For an overview of Kalbarri's marine life, visit the **Kalbarri Oceanarium** (tel: 08-9937 2027; daily 10am–4pm; admission charge) opposite the marina on the foreshore. Here you'll see ocean-dwelling creatures of all shapes and sizes in a variety of large aquariums and touch pools.

Fashion

In recent years, Perth designers have been making a mark on the national scene. The WA government has employed a grant scheme similar to the one that launched New Zealand's fashion industry, and it has generated much success locally. However, West Australian style, by and large, is fairly relaxed. Suits are rarely seen outside corporate offices, and in summer just about everyone goes about in a pair of thongs (flip-flops). Major international fashion trends are usually followed but with a watered-down edge. Generally speaking, high-street fashion here is more conservative than on the east coast.

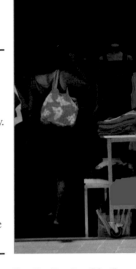

Designer

Adam Heath

Bayview Terrace, Claremont; tel: 08-9385 1044; www.adam heath.com.au; Mon–Sat 9am–5.30pm, Thur until 9pm; train: Claremont; bus: 98 and 99 to Gugeri Street.

Located in the new Claremont Quarter shopping precinct, Adam Heath is a magnet for local fashionistas. In store you'll find DVF, Marc by Marc Jacobs, Akira, Megan Park and more.

Keep an eye out for the **Perth Fashion Festival**. It usually takes place in September and is widely covered in the daily newspaper, *The West Australian*, as well as *The Sunday Times*. There are a number of free public events, showcasing local designers and models, plus many events where you can buy a ticket for entry. Many of Australia's top models come from Perth, including the internationally famous Gemma Ward, who has worked for just about every big fashion house, including Hermes, Prada, Calvin Klein, Burberry and Karl Lagerfeld.

SEE SHOPPING, P.111

Dilettante

575 Wellington Street; tel: 08-9322 2717; Tue–Thur 10am–5.30pm, Fri until 8pm, Sat 10am–5pm, Sun noon–5pm; train: Perth; map p.134 A3

Dilettante stocks some of the world's edgier designers, including Vivienne Westwood, Luella and Rick Owens. These fashions are expensive and quirky, and definitely for those who aren't afraid to stand out (leather shirt, anyone?).

Elle Boutique

56 Weld Street, Nedlands; tel: 08-9386 6868; www.elleonline.com.au; Mon–Fri 10am–5.30pm, Thur until 8pm, Sat 10am–5pm, Sun noon–5pm; bus: 99 to Doonan Road

When it comes to fabulous fashion, there's nowhere hotter than Elle Boutique where owner Wendy Marshall has built a reputation both at home and abroad as Perth's leading trendsetter. Find Chloe, Stella McCartney, Lanvin and more.

Parker & Co.

Shop 207 Trinity Arcade, off Hay Street Mall; tel: 08-9321 8621; www.parkerco.com.au;

Mon–Thur 10am–5pm, Fri until 8pm, Sat 10am–5pm, Sun noon–5pm; train: Perth; map p.134 A2

Parker & Co. specialises in the top end of men's clothing, especially suiting. Labels include Paul Smith, Zegna, Acqua di Palma and several Italian labels. Stores can also be found at Claremont Quarter, and on St Georges Terrace and Murray Street in the City.

Varga Girl

148 Oxford Street, Leederville; tel: 08-9444 8990; Mon, Tue and Sat 9.30am–5.30pm, Wed and Fri until 6pm, Thur until 9pm, Sun 11am–5pm; train: Leederville

The place to come for unusual designs that won't terrify you (but they might shock your credit card). Varga Girl is always keen to support local designers, and also has a good range of New Zealand fashion. You'll find Perth's 'it' designer, Aurelio Costarella, stocked here.

Zomp

2 Bay View Terrace, Claremont; tel: 08-9384 6250; www.zomp.com.au; Mon–Sat 10am–6pm, Fri until 9pm, Sun noon–5pm; train: Claremont

Left: shopping in the sunshine.

8282; www.sportsgirl.com.au; Mon–Thur 9am–5.30pm, Fri until 9pm, Sat 9am–5pm, Sun noon– 5pm; train: Perth; map p.134 A2

For high-turnover, reasonably priced, trend-focused fashion, you can't beat Sportsgirl. There are finds to be had for all ages, so don't be put off by the hordes of youngsters shopping to their budget. Their accessories are great.

Target
Hay Street Mall; tel: 08-9327 3700; www.target.com.au; Mon–Thur 8am–6pm, Fri until 9pm, Sat 9–5pm, Sun noon– 5.30pm; train: Perth; map p.134 A2

Target has been seen as the poor cousin to just about everything, but in the last year its collaboration with big-name designers creating capsule ranges (Stella McCartney, Josh Goot, Zac Posen) has seen people look at the store with fresh eyes. While much still can be passed over, you will find good items here, especially in the younger women's wear.

Below: taking a break from shopping.

Perth's best shoe shop, stocking international labels such as Ixus and Costume National as well as bargains like Anna Vanilla, where a pair of leopard-print slippers will only set you back A$55. Also at: 47 King Street; tel: 08-9321 0765; Mon–Sat 9.30am–5.30pm, Fri until 5pm, Sun noon–5pm; train: Perth City; map p.134 A2

Inexpensive
Country Road
307 Murray Street; tel: 08-9321 3700; www.countryroad.com.au; Mon–Thur 10am–5.30pm, Fri until 8pm, Sat 9.30am–5pm, Sun noon–5pm; train: Perth; map p.134 A2

Don't be fooled by the name: there is no 'country' style in Country Road's clothing. The ranges are moderately priced, decent quality and trend-focused without being too edgy. They are strong across clothes for women, men, children and for homewear. Stores can be found across Perth and the city store has a café worth visiting.

Harbour Town
840 Wellington Street; tel: 08-9321 2282; www.harbour

town.com.au; Mon–Thur 9am–5.30pm, Fri until 9pm, Sat 9am–5pm, Sun noon–5pm; train: City West; bus: yellow CAT to Harbour Town; map p.133 E3

Factory-price bargains make it worth taking a trip to this outlet shopping centre. Built on the site of an old produce market, Harbour Town's dozens of stores sell discontinued lines, end-of-season stock and some current ranges.

Picnic
80 Rokeby Road, Subiaco; tel: 08-9381 2722; www.picniccloth ing.com.au; Mon–Wed 9am–5.30pm, Thur until 8pm, Fri–Sat 9am–5pm, Sun 11am–5pm; train: Subiaco; map p.132 B3

The Picnic chain is Perth-owned and offers a safer, slightly more mature take on trends you'll see in younger fashion stores. Pricing is very reasonable, and you will be able to pick up some good basics too. Picnic has other stores across the city. Visit the website for store locations.

Sportsgirl
709 Hay Street; tel: 08-9481

Festivals and Events

Summer weather is so reliable that you can exhaust yourself trying to get out there and see everything that is on offer. When the weather is cooler there is less on, as West Australians don't tend to react well to the cold or the very little rain that falls, and tend to stay indoors unless there is a game of AFL football to attend. Nevertheless, there are still things to see year-round. As Perth grows in profile it is attracting more and more big events, and there are more being put on by enthusiastic local bodies.

January–February

Perth Cup
Generally New Year's Day; www.perthracing.com.au
A horse-racing carnival and Perth's premier fashion event. Lots of champagne, posh frocks and outrageous hats.

Australia Day Skyworks
26 January; www.perth.wa.gov.au/skyworks/
Huge display of fireworks exploding off barges on the Swan River and the tops of the city's skyscrapers. It is the country's largest Australia Day public celebration, attracting a larger crowd than any other city's festivities.

Perth International Arts Festival
February; www.perthfestival.com.au
Longest-established annual arts festival in the southern hemisphere, with artists from all cultural fields attending from all over the world. This festival is beginning to be considered by performers to be as relevant as big festivals such as the Edinburgh event. The festival covers theatre, dance, music (contemporary and classical),

free public events and film.

The film component runs from December through to March and takes place at two locations. The first, the **Somerville auditorium**, is an open-air cinema at the University of Western Australia. The tradition is to bring a picnic, grab a low-slung deck-chair and enjoy the film in the open air. You are surrounded by tall pines, which create a theatre-like effect. The second location is at **Joondalup Pines**, a similar outdoor venue. Both cine-

mas screen films from around the world, which you won't get to see at any other cinema in Perth.

Rottnest Channel Swim
February; www.rottnestchannelswim.com.au
On a Saturday in mid-February, around 10,000 swimmers take to the water off Cottesloe Beach and swim the 20km (12.4 miles) to Rottnest Island. The departure and arrival are both worth seeing as a spectator, and the party on Rottnest afterwards is something to behold.
SEE ALSO SPORTS, P.115

March–May

Sculpture by the Sea
March; www.sculpturebythesea.com
A free outdoor sculpture exhibition featuring innovative art, set on and around Cottesloe Beach. Attracts around 60,000 visitors.

Fremantle Street Arts Festival
Easter; www.fremantlefestivals.com

Left: at the Perth Cup.

Left: surfing at Margaret River's Main Break.

wheels tackle WA's remote and rugged terrain.

Kings Park Wild Flower Festival
September and October
The festival shows off a huge range of WA's native flowers.

Gay Pride March
Generally October; www.pridewa.asn.au
A colourful gay and lesbian parade through the streets of Northbridge.
SEE ALSO GAY AND LESBIAN, P.63

Perth Fashion Festival
September; www.perthfashion festival.com.au
This style extravaganza is emerging as one of Australia's most dynamic fashion festivals, featuring more than 50 runway shows, parades and fashion events.

Royal Show
Early October; www.perthroyal show.com.au
The Royal showcases vast WA resources, agriculture and industry, plus all the fun of the fair in Sideshow Alley.

November–December

Awesome Children's Festival
November; www.awesomearts.com
This 10-day family event is filled with performances and installations that will entertain and enchant children in a wide range of age groups.
SEE ALSO CHILDREN, P.36

Hyundai Hopman Cup
Late December–early January; www.hopmancup.com
An invitational mixed tennis tournament drawing many of the world's best players – Serena Williams, Roger Federer and Justine Henin to name just a few who have been on centre court.

Public Holidays
New Year's Day: 1 Jan
Australia Day: 26 Jan
Labor Day: 1st Mon in Mar
Anzac Day: 25 Apr
Good Friday: Mar/Apr
Easter Monday: Mar/Apr
Foundation Day: 1st Mon in June
Queen's Birthday: 1st Mon in Oct
Christmas Day: 25 Dec
Boxing Day: 26 Dec
New Year's Eve: 31 Dec

Entertainment with the skills and outrageous behaviour of the world's best buskers.

Drug Aware Margaret River Pro
April; www.drugawarepro.com
A world-qualifying surfing event that attracts some of the world's best surfers to Margaret River's Main Break.

June–July

York Gourmet Food and Wine Festival
Early June; www.yorkwa.org
Fresh produce, interactive cooking demonstrations, balloon artists and face painters will entertain the whole family in the majestic York Town Hall in the picturesque Avon Valley.

Mundaring Truffle Festival
End of July; www.mundaring trufflefestival.com
This truffle-themed weekend, held in the picturesque Perth Hills, offers a host of gourmet experiences including food tastings and markets as well as truffle cooking demonstrations.

August

City to Surf
Late August
This is the largest community sporting event in Western Australia incorporating a marathon, half marathon, a 12km (7.4-mile) run/walk and a 4km (2.5-mile) run/walk/wheelchair. Starting in the city centre, runners pass by Kings Park before ending at stunning City Beach.

September–October

Australasian Safari
Late September; www.australasiansafari.com.au
The toughest endurance motor-sport event in the Asia Pacific region, this ultimate off-road adventure sees competitors on two and four

55

Film

W hile Perth doesn't have the large film production industry that Sydney does, the city's isolation and status as the capital of Western Australia, with its unique landscapes, have seen it develop a healthy industry that is well supported by the WA government through grants. The industry can and does support some producers, directors, actors and crew in a full-time capacity. Many local people are also movie buffs, and there is a healthy range of alternatives to the mainstream multiplexes; in summer, several outdoor cinemas run for several months, taking advantage of the good weather.

Perth's Film Industry

Western Australia's rugged and varied landscape has attracted productions from around Australia. Big-name Australian director Philip Noyce, whose better-known films include *Clear and Present Danger*, *The Saint*, *The Bone Collector*, *Patriot Games*, *Dead Calm* and *Newsfront*, shot in WA in 2002 when filming *Rabbit-Proof Fence*, which tells the story, based on a true event,

of three Aboriginal children who, when taken from their parents as part of the 'Stolen Generation' *(see Aboriginal Culture, p.26)*, flee and walk home along the 1,500km (932-mile) rabbit-proof fence. The fence was installed in the 1930s with the hope that it would keep the devastating rabbit population from encroaching across the country.

Other films, such as the 2006 psychological thriller *Last Train to Freo*, directed by actor Jeremy Sims, and *Japanese Story*, starring Toni Collette, were produced in Western Australia, and in 2008 Baz Luhrmann's epic *Australia*, starring Nicole Kidman and Hugh Jackman, was filmed in the north of the state.

The most recent silver screen success to come out of WA is director Kriv Stender's *Red Dog* (released 2011). Starring Rachel Taylor and Josh Lucas, the film is based on the true story of the red cloud kelpie (Red Dog) who united a local community while roaming

the Australian outback in search of his lost master.

One of Perth's most famous exports was actor Heath Ledger. Ledger, who died in 2008, grew up in Perth, attending the prestigious Guildford Grammar. Ledger was first noticed on the Australian film scene in 1997 with *Blackrock* and *Two Hands*. After breaking into Hollywood with *A Knight's Tale* and *10 Things I Hate about You*, Ledger featured in some underwhelm-

Below: actor Heath Ledger (1979–2008).

ScreenWest, the state's film funding body, receives over A$4 million each year from Lotterywest. Lotterywest is responsible for running cash lotteries in WA, but unlike in other states, Lotterywest is a not-for-profit organisation, and redistributes around A$145 million each year back into the community through a wide variety of grants. With part of its funding, ScreenWest is implementing a five-year Indigenous Screen Strategy (2010-15) designed to support, strengthen and grow this burgeoning sector of the local market.

Left: the acclaimed film *Rabbit-Proof Fence*.

Enjoy a twilight picnic, followed by a film under the stars. Moonlight Cinema in Kings Park's Synergy Parklands (www.moonlight.com.au) is a favourite. From December to March it screens a combination of latest releases, and contemporary, cult and classic movies. There's a candy bar on site, but movie-goers often prefer to bring their own basket packed with cheese, crackers, wine and other goodies. Beanbag chairs are available for hire – get there early and bring a blanket.

ing roles, before Ang Lee's *Brokeback Mountain* saw him commended with an Oscar nomination. His tragic and sudden death at the age of 28 saw the world's paparazzi descending on Cottesloe Beach for his funeral. Ledger's family still lives in Perth.

Cinemas

Many cinemas in Perth offer a cheap-ticket day each week, usually Tuesday but sometimes Wednesday; check with each cinema.

The Astor
659 Beaufort Street, Mount Lawley; tel: 08-9370 1777; www.astorcinema.com.au; daily from 10am; bus: 67, 21
Heritage-listed Art Deco building showing modern and classic films.

Camelot Outdoor Cinema
16 Lochee Street, Mosman Park; tel: 08-9385 4793; www.luna palace.com.au; daily from 10am; bus: 103
An Art Deco building with theatre space. Cinema is in a garden, with deckchairs, a bar and food available. You may BYO food, but not alcohol.

Cinema Paradiso
164 James Street, Northbridge; tel: 08-9227 1771; www.luna palace.com.au; daily from 10am; train: Perth; bus: blue CAT; map p.134 A3
Shows a mix of art-house films, often subtitled.

Luna Cinema
155 Oxford Street, Leederville; tel: 08-9444 4056; www.luna palace.com.au; daily from 10am; train: Leederville
Luna has one large cinema, many small studios and an outdoor one for summer, where there's a bar and you can bring a picnic. Luna also runs several festivals throughout the year, including a Manga (Japanese animation) one and a Bollywood one. Each Monday night a different 'double' is screened, starting at 7.30pm. If you can stay up late on a Monday night, it's great value.

Somerville Auditorium
University of WA, Nedlands; tel: 08-9488 1732; www.perth festival.com/lotterywestfestival films; Dec–Mar: doors open around 6.30pm; bus: 102, 103; map p.136 A2

This is the main venue for films screened during the Perth International Arts Festival; there's another at the Joondalup campus of Edith Cowan University. Somerville is very atmospheric with deckchairs lined up under tall pine trees.

The Windsor
98 Stirling Highway, Nedlands; tel: 08-9386 3554; www.luna palace.com.au; daily from 10am; bus: 102, 103
A two-cinema Art Deco building that invokes the grand age of cinema.

Below: the Luna Cinema.

57

Food and Drink

Stereotypically, Perth is thought of as the country cousin to Australia's cosmopolitan centres of Sydney and Melbourne. However, thanks to successive waves of immigration from all over the world, an abundance of fresh produce and the wealth from a sustained resources boom, Perth's food has come into its own in recent years, while the riches of the Margaret River vineyards also add splendid wines to this mix. A new wave of dynamic chefs enthusiastic about local produce means that you will find a brand of modern Australian cuisine in Perth that easily ranks alongside that found elsewhere in the country.

Origins and Influences

Although Western Australia's first settlers went to the trouble of establishing the state's first vineyards in the Swan Valley, Western Australian cuisine remained defiantly British until well into the 1950s. The first inklings of a Mediterranean influence developed in the 1920s when many Italian and Slavic immigrants arrived, and flourished in the post-war immigration boom. However, it is only since Asian immigration, the advent of fusion cuisine and the food revolution of the 1980s that Australia developed the dynamic cuisine that defines the country today.

Such is the profusion of flavours in contemporary Perth that you would have to scour the myriad menus to find anything akin to the traditional British old-style cuisine of yesteryear. These days a roast of prime Western Australian lamb is more likely to have a Moroccan, Mediterranean or Indian mien, and fish dishes will, in all probability, be accented with Thai or Vietnamese flavours. Even the good old Aussie pavlova has taken a back seat to desserts such as black sticky rice pudding or coconut fried ice cream. From risottos to rotis,

sambals to sausages, almost every element of every national cuisine is reinvented on Perth menus every week.

Perth Cuisine

POPULAR DISHES

Western Australians love fresh seafood, so ocean fare is a local favourite. Local food ambassadors Kate Lamont, owner of Lamont's Bishop's House in the CBD and Lamont's Cottesloe; and Chris Taylor of Fraser's Restaurant in Kings Park, create menus that make the most of WA's fresh ocean produce. Practically every restaurant in town will have a fish of the day, from the

Below: fresh fruit on offer at the Station Street Markets in Subiaco.

Left: a beautifully prepared lobster dish at Fraser's Restaurant *(see p.100)*.

state offering a unique blend of extra virgin olive oil.

Locally grown persimmons, tamarillos and tropical fruits have joined a long list of staples, such as stone fruits, apples, pears and myriad Asian vegetables, that are sought after at home and in Southeast Asia. New Norcia panforte and biscotti are exported all over the world. Locally made chocolates and preserves also compete with overseas imports, and there is an array of artisan yoghurts. But as an example of the much-vaunted West Australian audacity, the local black truffles that are now appearing on Perth tables would have to win hands down.

Eating In

If there's anything Perthites enjoy more than dining out, it is eating in, and being invited to someone's home is the best compliment you can receive. Home cooking has also undergone a revolution in Perth in recent years, where dishes such as beef rendang, green curry and couscous have taken their place alongside roasts, stews and grills. Long, hot summers ensure that the barbecue is a local institution, while picnics are an essential component of an outing to an outdoor cinema *(see Film, p.57)*.

If someone invites you to bring a chop for the barbie, you can be assured they mean a dozen or more well-marinated chops. Understatement is as Australian as BYO (bring your own wine/beer), and local custom decrees you never turn up for a meal at someone's house without a bottle of good wine.

Northbridge is the place to come to find many of the world's cuisines in one district: during the day you can pop between Italian, Indian, Chinese, Vietnamese and European bakers, butchers and provedores. At night these places close and are taken over by restaurants serving meals in these cuisines.

morning's catch. A long-time crowd pleaser are the garlic prawns at **The Witch's Cauldron** *(see p.105)*, which have been served unchanged at this Subiaco restaurant for 30 years. Degustation menus, as presented at top restaurants such as **Jacksons** *(see p.104)*, **Restaurant Amuse** *(see p.102)* and **The Loose Box** *(see p.107)*, are increasing in popularity.

LOCAL PRODUCE AND ARTISAN FOODS

A key feature of local cuisine is its excellent produce. Long renowned for high-quality lamb, beef and wheat, as well as for fish, fruit and vegetables, the state has seen a

massive increase in the production of gourmet produce in recent years. Boutique bakeries, artisan and organic butchers and speciality cheesemakers thrive thanks to an upsurge of public interest in food, not to mention a 30-year-long resources boom that has seen sustained growth levels significantly higher than the national average. Little wonder, then, that locally produced Wagyu beef at A$120 per kilo is finding its way onto Perth's most discerning tables; or that Kervella artisan goat's cheese is now a staple on many a restaurant and café menu. The superbly succulent and tender Arkady Farm lamb is beloved of the finest east-coast eateries. Farmed barramundi and trout have now joined marron, rock lobster, Patagonian toothfish, sardines, dhufish and snow crab at the table. Shellfish is varied and abundant, and even Japanese chefs are demanding Margaret River venison.

Boutique olive oil production is at an all-time high, with almost every region in the

Above: picnicking in the Swan Valley on a sunny day.

Where to Buy Food

Boatshed Market
40 Jarrad Street, Cottesloe; tel: 08-9284 5176; www.boatshed market.com.au; daily 6.30–8pm; train: Cottesloe; bus: 102, 103
The Boatshed is a foodie's delight. Inside you will find a fishmonger, butcher, bakehouse and deli. All offer top-quality products; the cheese counter in particular always has a fantastic selection. Samples are available throughout the store, and the ready-made meals are very good, as is the quality and range of the fresh produce. There is also a florist and a large range of gourmet groceries.

The Black Truffle
82 Stirling Highway, North Fremantle; tel: 08-9336 1796; www.theblacktruffle.com.au; daily 7am–7pm; train: North Fremantle; bus: 102
This gourmet newcomer has quickly become a reliable venue for discerning foodies in the Freo area. It's a providore and delicatessen, selling boutique and otherwise hard to find groceries, and there is a great selection of cheese, antipasti, charcuterie and ready-made meals. The coffee is great too.

Chez Jean-Claude Patisserie
333 Rokeby Road, Subiaco; tel: 08-9381 7968; www.chez jeanclaudepatisserie.com.au; Mon–Fri 6am–6pm; train: Subiaco; map p.132 B2
This is a little slice of baking heaven on the far end of Rokeby Road. It does a roaring trade in rolls, sandwiches, pies, sweet treats and cakes produced by French-Swiss baker Jean-Claude. There's no seating, but it's so good you won't mind taking away.

David Jones Foodhall
622 Hay Street Mall; tel: 08-9210 4000; www.davidjones. com.au; Mon–Wed 9.30am–7pm, Thur–Fri 9.30am–9pm, Sat 9am–5pm, Sun 11am–5pm; train: Perth; map p.134 A2
Located on the ground floor of Perth's swishest department store, the David Jones Foodhall is a magnet for any foodie. Aside from the produce available for purchase, there is an oyster bar serving fresh and cooked oysters with champagne, a sushi bar, a noodle and curry bar (serving a top-notch pad thai), fresh sandwiches, a coffee and chocolate bar and a fresh juice bar. Take some time

out from shopping to relax with some top-quality food.
SEE ALSO SHOPPING, P.109

The Earth Market
14/375 Hay Street, Subiaco; tel: 08-9382 2266; Mon–Sat 9am–5pm; train: Subiaco; map p.132 B3
This shop-cum-café specialises in whole and organic foods. Come here to buy organic veg and a wide range of healthy options.

Fremantle Markets
Cnr South Terrace and Henderson Street; www.fremantle markets.com.au; Fri 9am–8pm, Sat–Sun and Mon public holidays 9am–6pm; train: Fremantle
Complete with fruit and vegetables, seafood, freshly baked bread, cheeses, coffees, herbs and spices and gourmet foods.
SEE ALSO SHOPPING, P.110

Kailis Bros Fish Market
101 Oxford Street, Leederville; tel: 08-9443 6300; www.kailis brosleederville.com.au; daily 8am–6pm; train: Leederville
Kailis is just about the biggest seafood supplier in WA. Their public fish market is beautiful; choose from a wide range of whole fish, mussels, oysters, crabs, lobster, scallops and other seasonal delights on ice beds, plus filleted fish, mari-

nated and pre-made mixes. They also stock a small range of cookery books, knives, bread and small goods.
SEE ALSO RESTAURANTS, P.102

Kakulas Bros
183 William Street, Northbridge; tel: 08-9328 5285; www.kakulas bros.com.au; Mon–Sat 8am–6pm; train: Perth; map p.134 A3

A stalwart on the Perth food scene; come here for bargain prices on bulk produce. They stock a huge range of Continental ingredients.

Mondo's Butchers
824 Beaufort Street, Inglewood; tel: 08-9371 6350; www.mondo. net.au; Tue–Fri 8am–6pm, Sat 7am–2pm; bus: 67, 21

Vince Garreffa is a local legend. He has recently revamped Mondo's Butchers, expanding his extensive range of meat to include ready-to-cook meals such as gourmet pies and quiches (all made on site without preservatives and with top-quality meat), vacuum-sealed meats such as emu, kangaroo and crocodile; bread and home essentials. Vince is the man behind White Rocks veal, which is favoured by the country's top chefs.

The Re Store
231 Oxford Street, Leederville; tel: 08-9444 9644; Mon–Sat 8am–6pm, Sat 8am–5pm; train: Perth; map p.134 A3

The Re Store is a joy, selling Italian meats, cheeses, sweets, bread and more. The Leederville branch has a liquor store with a very good range and good prices, and also a counter where you can have fresh rolls filled with a range of fillings. Also at: 231 Oxford Street, Leederville; tel: 08-9444 9644; train: Leederville

Station Street Markets
41 Station Street, Subiaco; tel: 08-9382 2832; www.subiaco markets.com; Fri, Sun 9am–5.30pm; train: Subiaco; map p.132 B4

A large, cheap range of fresh fruit and veg. There are also shops selling bulk groceries such as nuts, cereals, rice and so on, as well as an excellent French baker.
SEE ALSO SHOPPING, P.110

Torre Butchers
41–3 Lake Street, Northbridge; tel: 08-9328 8317; www.torre. com.au; Mon–Sat 7am–5pm; train: Perth; bus: blue CAT; map p.134 A3

Torre is known as one of the best butchers in town. They

Currently, Perthites are getting back to basics and embracing the slow food movement – both at home and at restaurants. Check out www.slowfoodperth.org.au for a list of local farmers markets and slow feed events.

have a wide selection of hard-to-find meats and can offer expert advice as well as prep them for you.

Tran's Emporium
358 Newcastle Street, North-bridge; tel: 08-9228 3099; www.tafc.com.au; daily 8am–6pm; train: Perth; bus: blue CAT; map p.134 A4

As the name suggests, you'll find a large range at Tran's. It is a specialist Asian supplier, so come here for unusual pastes, sauces and hard-to-find veg. There are also Asian cooking implements, crockery and other interesting items.

La Vigna
302 Walcott Street, Mount Lawley; tel: 08-9271 1907; www.lavigna.com.au; Mon–Sat 10am–8pm; bus: 67, 21

Mike Tamburri has one of the finest wine collections around; if you want good advice and a great range, this is the place.

Below: fresh fish on offer at Kailis Bros Fish Market.

Gay and Lesbian

Perth's gay scene is minor compared to a city such as Sydney, where gay couples can interact in exactly the same way as straight couples. Perth, in many respects, remains a conservative community, and while homophobia is mostly a thing of the past, gay couples do not enjoy the same sense of confidence that is found in other big cities. Having said that, the gay community is alive and well, with a few select popular hangouts. The favoured and most tolerant hang-outs for gay and lesbian locals and visitors are mostly in the inner city, such as Northbridge, Highgate and Mount Lawley.

Accommodation

These hotels are the most gay-friendly, or in the case of Pension of Perth, gay-owned and operated.

Hotel Northbridge
210 Lake Street, Northbridge; tel: 08-9328 5254; www.hotel northbridge.com.au; $$; bus: red or blue CAT; map p.134 B4
This beautiful old building has been restored and now sports lovely rooms kept in style with the era of the building. Downstairs is a popular restaurant and bar, and the hotel is only a short stroll to Hyde Park in the north and Perth city to the south. It is out of the noise of Northbridge and is situated on a tree-lined, mainly residential street.

Pension of Perth
3 Throssell Street; tel: 08-9228 9049; www.pensionperth.

Price categories are for a standard double room per night without breakfast.
$$$$ = A$250 plus
$$$ = A$175–$250
$$ = A$100–$175
$ = under A$100

com.au; $$; bus: red or blue CAT
Run by a gay couple, this bed and breakfast offers comfortable, cosy accommodation and a relaxed atmosphere for those seeking something more personal than a big hotel.
SEE ALSO HOTELS, P.70

Sullivans Hotel Perth
166 Mounts Bay Road, Perth; tel: 08-9321 8022; www.sullivans.com.au; $$; train: Perth; map p.133 E1
A small, boutique family-owned hotel, Sullivans is located next to Kings Park and the Convention Centre, a 1.5 km (1-mile) walk to the CBD and a short bus ride to Northbridge. The staff are gay-friendly and will make stays in Perth comfortable for gay and lesbian clientele.

Venues

Connections Nightclub
81 James Street, Northbridge; tel: 08-9328 5166; www.connectionsnightclub.com; Wed, Sat 10pm–late; map p.134 A3
Connections (or 'Connies' as it's affectionately known), is Australia's longest-running

gay and lesbian nightclub, with more than 30 years of fabulous tunes and high heels behind it. Renovated for its 30th birthday, Connies is now resplendent in marble and mirrors, and has a small rooftop garden with city skyline views.

The Court Hotel
50 Beaufort Street; tel: 08-9328 5292; www.thecourt.com.au; daily noon–late; bus: blue CAT to Aberdeen Street Art Centre; map p.134 B3
The Court Hotel has recently

Left: hitting the streets for the annual Pride Parade.

Festival marks a big week in the gay and lesbian calendar (with the exception of 2007, when amid talk of unpaid debts, no festival was held). The Pride Parade, held on a Saturday night, is not nearly as big as Sydney's Mardi Gras, but is still a night for celebration and attracts as much of a straight crowd as it does a gay and lesbian crowd. Visit the website to check for updates.

Safety

Perth is a reasonably safe place to live and visit, with very few homophobic incidents, but it is always wise to stay alert to the possibility of running into people with prejudices, especially once out of the city. Generally speaking, as is usual elsewhere, attitudes in the countryside are more conservative. In Perth, many local people may not be as used to seeing open displays of affection between gay and lesbian couples as in some other cities, but by the same token, the population is generally well educated and tolerant.

In the main, being openly gay rarely causes problems. However, at night in some districts where heavy drinking occurs at weekends (Northbridge, for example), it is advisable to steer clear of large groups of drunk men.

had several million spent on a revamp, and now has an impressive bar, along with an outdoor pizzeria and other areas. At weekends the place heaves until the small hours and often a fabulous drag show is the highlight of the night. There is also a restaurant which has received good reviews. Straight-friendly, too.

Honey Lounge Bar
11/663 Newcastle Street, Leederville; Tue–Sat 7pm–late; train: Leederville

Perth's newest gay bar is a

fabulous, laid-back venue filled with ottomans, lounges, gold picture frames and reprints of classic works of art. Designed to be frisky and fun, the venue welcomes the entire gay community and hosts live shows, cabaret performances and DJs on a purpose-built stage.

Perth Steamworks
369 William Street, Northbridge; tel: 08-9328 2930; www.perth steamworks.com.au; daily noon–late; bus: blue CAT to William Street; map p.134 B4

This steamworks has a six-man pool, dry sauna and steam room. It's a popular hang-out in which to relax, or for meeting men who might be interested in slightly more. There are fetish rooms, private cubicles and plenty of condoms and information regarding safe sex.

Festivals

Pride
www.pridewa.asn.au
Each year, October's Pride

Left: the gay-friendly Pension of Perth bed and breakfast.

History and Architecture

50,000 BC
Aborigines populate all of Australia.

1606
First authenticated voyage to Australia, by the Dutch ship the *Duyfken* ('Little Dove').

1616
Dutch explorer Dirk Hartog in the Eendracht makes first authenticated landing in Western Australia, at Shark Bay.

1696–7
Discovery of Swan River by Willem de Vlamingh.

1826
King George Sound is occupied by convicts from Sydney under Major Lockyer.

1828
British government approves founding of Swan River Colony; appoints Captain Stirling lieutenant-governor.

1829
Formal possession of the colony is taken by Captain Fremantle; in June Stirling arrives to found the colony. Pitched, corrugated-iron roofs are the norm in residential housing and as architecture is dictated by climate, verandas are popular as they keep the houses cooler.

1831
Stirling made governor. King George Sound convict settlement is withdrawn. First newspaper issued.

1843
Petitions for the introduction of convicts.

1850
Convicts sent from Britain to meet labour shortage and help build Perth.

1856
Queen Victoria grants Perth city status. Gothic Revival-style architecture dominates churches and cathedrals.

1868
Convict transportation ends.

1870
Colony gains representative government.

1871
Municipalities Act and Elementary Education Act passed; first private railway built.

1877
Telegraph links Perth and London via Adelaide.

1881
Eastern railway links Perth, Fremantle and Guildford.

1886
Kimberley goldfield proclaimed, the first of several in Western Australia.

1890
WA gains responsible government. Sir John Forrest forms first government.

1892
Construction of Fremantle Harbour begins.

1893
Paddy Hannan's Kalgoorlie find becomes 'The Golden Mile', and the gold rush transforms Perth.

1899
Women get the vote, ahead of Britain, Canada and the US. Perth Electric Tramway begins to supersede horse transport. The Boer War breaks out and 1,231 WA men go to South Africa; 126 die, one wins the Victoria Cross. Back in Perth, the building of the Goldfields Water Supply commences (completed January 1903). Towns are seeing the pay-off from the gold rush, with their public buildings becoming grander and more embellished. Today these buildings are usually pubs.

1901
Commonwealth of Australia inaugurated 1 January. WA becomes a state of federal Australia.

1901
WA joins the British Empire. Duke of York visits Perth and names Kings Park.

1911
University of Western Australia opens. Homes are 'federation' style; there are still many examples of this in areas such as Mount Lawley.

1914–18
6,000 Western Australians die and thousands more are wounded in World War I.

1917
Trans-Australian Railway links WA to eastern states.

1920S
Fremantle is busiest oil-fuelling port in Australia; world's first long-distance air service operates from Perth centre.

1929
Amid centenary celebrations of the 1829 founding, George V declares Perth a 'Lord Mayoralty', and Fremantle becomes a city.

1931
The Great Depression results in one in four Perth men being jobless; a 5,000-strong protest march ends in violence and arrests.

1933
State of WA votes to opt out of federation, but the UK government rules the move 'unconstitutional'.

1939–45
Perth men and women serve in World War II; city prepares for air raids. Fremantle is essential to the war effort, as the secret base for 170 Allied submarines. Sunderland and Catalina flying boats are based on the Swan. Victory in the Pacific on 15 August 1945 (VP Day).

1954–8
More of the Swan River reclaimed for building of the Narrows Bridge and Freeway.

1959
First television service begins.

1962
Perth hosts Empire Games.

1968
Worst tremors in memory rock Perth as Meckering, 130km (80 miles) east of the city, is destroyed by an earthquake.

1971
Concert Hall opens, deemed as important an icon as the Town Hall (1870).

1978
HMAS *Stirling* is the naval base for Australia's submarine fleet.

1979
WA celebrates first 150 years.

1983
Australia II wins America's Cup off Rhode Island. It is the first non-American entrant to win.

1987
America's Cup held in Fremantle, putting the port city on the world map.

1999
World's earliest known life form, 3.5 billion-year-old stromatolites, found in outback and brought to Perth's WA Museum.

2001
Labor regains state power after eight years in opposition.

2004
Perth Convention Centre opens.

2008
Plans are unveiled for a new city waterfront development.

2009
Controversially, West Australians vote once and for all against daylight saving time.

2011
In February 64 homes are destroyed and another 32 badly damaged as bushfires ravage Perth Hills.

2012
Foundation Day, celebrated annually on the first Monday in June to commemorate the founding of the Swan River Colony, officially changes to Western Australia Day.

Hotels

Perth is a small city where you can stay in the very centre at moderate cost and walk easily to theatres, entertainments, the park and the river. However, easy travel on fast trains, clean, air-conditioned buses, smooth roads and relatively inexpensive taxis means you can stay at the beaches or in leafy suburbs if you prefer, and still quickly get into the centre of Perth and Fremantle. The city has a wide range of hotel options, from small boutique hotels through to international five-star chains, but there is often a shortage of rooms available, so be sure to book in advance of arrival.

Accomodation in Perth

If you crave full-service, luxury hotel accommodation there is little choice but the hotels on Adelaide Terrace, the city riverside and at Burswood. However, high-quality, clean accommodation is available in all price ranges, at moderately priced hotels, bed and breakfast houses, and even backpackers' hostels all across the metropolitan area.

Great value and lavish comfort can also be experienced at some bed and breakfast establishments. Generally speaking, the B&B accommodation tends to match the area. Alternatively, you could stay in a rural location in the Swan Valley or the Darling Ranges, which are still only 30 minutes from the city. Staying outside

Perth, even for a short time, is a fast way to get the feel of 'real Australia'.

Swan River and Kings Park

The Richardson Hotel Suites and Spa
32 Richardson Street; tel: 08-9217 8888; www.the richardson.com.au; $$$$; bus: red CAT; map p.133 D3
The Richardson is Perth's newest boutique hotel. Boasting a fine-dining restaurant, Opus, and one of Perth's best day spas, the hotel has a range of rooms available, plus pool and sauna. The Richardson has counted pop stars such as Pink and Christina Aguilera as guests, so they must be doing something right.
SEE ALSO PAMPERING, P.87

Riverview on Mount Street
42 Mount Street; tel: 08-9321 8963; www.riverviewperth. com.au; $$–$$$; bus: 103, 37; map p.133 E2
These serviced apartments are in a great location. Mount Street runs down one edge of Kings Park, and at the bottom (it is an incredibly steep

street) there is a pedestrian flyover that crosses the freeway, quickly depositing you at the top of St George's Terrace near the Mill Street intersection. At the bottom of the building is the very cool Bouchard café, which serves excellent food.

Wyndham Vacation Resort The Outram
32 Outram Street, West Perth; tel: 08-9322 4888; www.hotels. wyndhamvrap.com; $$$$; bus: red CAT; map p.133 D3
A chic, Parisian-style boutique hotel in trendy West Perth, a stone's throw from Kings Park and the heart of

Below: the Duxton hotel.

Left: great views and stylishly retro design at Rydges.

If you have left it late to book accommodation, a good website to try is **www.wotif.com.au**. Hotels advertise special room rates, and there are some bargains to be had. You can book here usually a couple of weeks in advance, but the closer to the day you are looking for, the better bargain you'll find. The only catch is you will have restricted choice, and hotel rooms in Perth, especially over weekends, can be hard to find.

the city. Gourmet breakfast is served daily on the terrace, evening hors d' oeuvres are served in the lounge. There's a bar, and rooms are modern and sleek. The two-bedroom deluxe rooms have fully equipped kitchens.

City Centre

Aarons All Suites Hotel
12 Victoria Avenue; tel: 08-9318 4444, toll-free: 1800-000 675; www.aaronssuites.com.au; $$; bus: red CAT; map p.134 B1
A range of modern, fully equipped apartments, with a a rooftop spa and a barbecue area. Very near the CBD and Adelaide Terrace and within walking distance of the river and shops.

Criterion Hotel Perth
560 Hay Street; tel: 08-9325 5155, toll-free: 1800-245 155; www.criterion-hotel-perth.com.au; $$; bus: red CAT; map p.134 B2
In a central location opposite the historic Perth Town Hall and housed in a beautifully restored Art Deco building in the main shopping area, with a 'British pub' in the basement.

Duxton
1 St George's Terrace; tel: 08-9261 8000, toll-free: 1800-681 118; www.perth.duxton hotels.com; $$$$; bus: blue CAT; map p.134 B1
Beautifully renovated hotel in a heritage building (not that you would know by looking at it), formerly Perth's old tax office. Close to the Perth Concert Hall, Swan River and shops, the Duxton is known for its lavish breakfast buffet.

Hyatt Regency Perth
99 Adelaide Terrace; tel: 08-9225 1234; www.perth.regency.hyatt.com; $$$$; bus: red CAT; map p.135 C1
Pool, tennis court, fitness centre, sauna and everything rightly expected of a 5-star hotel. You can do elegant dining or café-style, or prop up one of several bars. The food options here are very good, from the Singapore-colonial style of Joe's Oriental Diner to the revamped Café and the sublime Gershwin's fine dining. They serve a lovely high tea in the atrium-style seating area at weekends. Touring musicians often stay here. Close to river, shopping, CBD and entertainments.

Below: the Art Deco exterior of the Criterion Hotel.

Above: a sundowner by the sea.

Medina Grand Perth

33 Mounts Bay Road, Perth; tel: 08-9217 8000; www.medina. com.au/medina-grand-perth/hotel; $$$; bus: blue CAT; map p.134 A2

Situated on the site of the Perth Convention & Exhibition Centre in the heart of the CBD, this bright, modern boutique hotel offers a range of studio, one- and two-bedroom serviced apartments, a gymnasium, sauna, heated outdoor pool and a popular restaurant/bar.

The Melbourne

Cnr Hay and Milligan streets; tel: 08-9320 3333; www.melbourne hotel.com.au; $$–$$$; train: Perth; map p.133 E2

A boutique hotel located in the heart of the CBD, The Melbourne offers an alternative to the polished new hotels of the city. With 34 rooms restored to reflect the

hotel's gold rush-era period character, it also offers a public bar downstairs and dining in either M Café or the Melbourne Restaurant. The bar is popular on Friday night with the city's after-work crowd, so you can easily feel you are in the midst of things.

New Esplanade Hotel

18 The Esplanade; tel: 08-9325 2000; www.newesplanade. com.au; $$; bus: blue CAT; map p.134 A2

Close to the river and Barrack Street Jetty and within easy reach of city shopping. No restaurant, but breakfast is served in the Esplanade Café. Some suites have a full kitchen and river views.

Parmelia Hilton

14 Mill Street, Perth; tel: 08-9215 2000; www.hilton.com; $$$$; bus: blue CAT; map p.134 A2

Ideal for both business and leisure travellers, the Hilton is located across the road from the Perth Convention & Exhibition Centre and a stone's throw from King's Street and shopping malls. Its restaurant, The Globe, has a reputation for being one of Perth's best.

Quest West End

451 Murray Street; tel: 08-9480 3888, toll-free: 1800-334 033; www.questapartments.com.au; $$$; bus: red CAT; map p.133 E3

At the border of the CBD and the main shopping areas, with easy access to restaurants and entertainment in both the CBD and Northbridge, this offers modern apartments with full kitchens and an on-site gym.

Rydges

815 Hay Street; tel: 08-9263 1800, reservations: 1300-857 922; www.rydges.com; $$$; train: Perth; map p.134 A2

The Rydges hotel is conveniently located on the corner of Hay and King streets in the CBD and is a reasonably large hotel for such CBD convenience. The large rooms have recently been renovated in a modern-retro and tactile style; ask for a room on a high-numbered floor for spectacular views from the big windows. Downstairs is the very popular CBD Bar and Restaurant, which packs out on Friday nights.

Somerset St George's Terrace

2185 St George's Terrace; tel: 08-9226 3355; www.somerset. com; $$$; train: Perth; map p.134 A2

Located right in the heart of St George's Terrace, this boutique hotel recently upgraded all its rooms so, although small, they are modern with flat screen TVs and sophisticated decor. There's a bustling bar downstairs and trendy King's Street is across the road.

East Perth

Bailey's Parkside Hotel-Motel

150 Bennett Street, East Perth; tel: 08-9220 9555; www.baileys motel.com.au; $; bus: red or

> Price categories are for a standard double room per night without breakfast.
> $$$$ = A$250 plus
> $$$ = A$175–$250
> $$ = A$100–$175
> $ = under A$100

blue CAT; map p.135 C2
Homely hotel opposite park, within walking distance of the city centre. Comfy but basic units are complemented by an on-site swimming pool and barbecue. Restaurant serves 'home-style' cooking, and the room tariff includes a Continental breakfast.

Crown Metropol Perth
Great Eastern Highway, Crown Perth, Burswood; tel: 08-9362 7777; www.crownmetropol perth.com.au; $$$$; bus: 24, 296
Modern and affordable, this is a stylishly designed hotel with premium facilities including a fully equipped gym and outdoor pool. Plus, right next door is Crown Metropol Perth with its world-class restaurants, golf course, 24-hour casino and more.

Crown Promenade Perth
Great Eastern Highway, Crown Perth, Burswood; tel: 08-9362 7777; www. crownpromenade perth.com.au; $$$; bus: 24, 296
Modern and affordable, this is a stylishly designed hotel with premium facilities, including a fully equipped gymnasium and outdoor pool. Plus, right next door is

Above: having a pint in the M Cafe at The Melbourne.

Crown Metropol Perth with its excellent retaurant and many facilities *(see previous entry)*.

Mont Clare Boutique Apartments
190 Hay Street; tel: 08-9224 4300; www.montclare apartments.com; $$; bus: red CAT; map.135 C1
Near the Swan River, these stylish, bright apartments are in a good location, well served by local restaurants. Well-furnished apartments of various sizes, with a full kitchen and laundry, outdoor pool and gym.

Sebel Residence East Perth
60 Royal Street, East Perth; tel: 08-9223 2500, toll-free: 13 15 15; www.mirvachotels.com/ sebel-residence-east-perth; $$$; bus: red CAT; map p.135 D2
These stylish serviced apartments are located right on the Swan River in Claisebrook – the hub of trendy East Perth's entertainment precinct. Wifi is free throughout the hotel, there's a charge-back arrangement with local restaurants and cafés, and it has a well-equipped gym and heated swimming pool overlooking the river.

Northbridge
Hotel Northbridge
210 Lake Street, Northbridge; tel: 08-9328 5254; www.hotel northbridge.com.au; $$; bus: red

Below: in the bar at Rydges.

Be aware that in Australia a sign saying 'hotel' can simply mean a pub and is not necessarily an indication of accommodation, especially where grand old properties are concerned. It dates from the days when all pubs had rooms for rent and were often the only accommodation to be found in a town.

or blue CAT; map p.134 B4
Lovely rooms in a recently restored building. The hotel is quietly located on a tree-lined street yet is just a short stroll from the heart of Northbridge's entertainment precinct. Downstairs is a popular restaurant and bar.

Nomads Billabong Backpackers Resort
381 Beaufort Street; tel: 08-9328 7720; www.billabong resort.com.au; $; bus: 60, 67; map p.134 B4
Adjacent to Northbridge entertainment and restaurant area, this colourful and lively hostel has air-conditioning and modern facilities, a swimming pool and gym, as well as a free breakfast.

The Old Swan Barracks
6 Francis Street; tel: 08-9428 0000; www.theoldswan barracks.com; $; train: Perth; map p.134 B3
A backpackers' hostel that is close to the Cultural Centre, art gallery and museum, and the Northbridge entertainment and restaurant area. Has many facilities, including a pool table, a kitchen and a gym.

Pension of Perth
3 Throssell Street; tel: 08-9228 9049; www.pensionperth.com. au; $$; bus: 60
Quiet 1897-built federation-style house near Hyde Park; has seven master bedrooms with en suite (spa or bath), fine furnishings and French antiques. Silver-service breakfast is served in the lounge or by the swimming pool.
SEE ALSO GAY AND LESBIAN, P.62

Subiaco

8 Nicholson
8 Nicholson Road, Subiaco; tel: 08-9382 1881; www.8nicholson. com.au; $$$$; train: Subiaco; map p.132 A1
Chandeliers, high ceilings, top of the range linen and ultra chic decor make this luxury boutique bed and breakfast perfect for style-conscious travellers. A delicious breakfast is included in the tariff and restaurants and shopping are a short stroll away.

Darby Park Subiaco
222 Hay Street; tel: 08-9380 0800; www.darbypark.com.au/ subiaco; $$$; train: Subiaco;

map p.132 C3
In cosmopolitan Subiaco with boutique shops, interesting restaurants and bars, and the Regal Theatre nearby. The one-, two- and three-bedroom apartments have full kitchens and laundry facilities. There's an outdoor pool, spa and barbecues, and The Vic bar and restaurant is part of the complex. It is also within spitting distance of Subiaco Oval, so when there is a game of AFL or rugby on you will be in the centre of it.

Fremantle

Bannister Suites
22 Bannister Street, Fremantle; tel: 08-9435 1288; www.bannistersuitesfreman-tle.com.au; $$$; train: Fremantle
A new, intimate boutique hotel located in the heart of 'Freo'. Comprises sixteen one- and two-bedroom luxury suites, and 14 studio rooms. They all have free broadband, LCD TVs and queen-size beds. Suites all have private lounge areas, coffee machines and kitchenettes.

Left: internet access is often offered at backpackers' hostels.

Accommodation in Perth's hotels is the tightest market in Australia at the moment, so don't wait until you get there to try and get a room. Make sure you book ahead, unless you are happy to try your luck at back-packers' if you don't have any joy at the city's larger hotels.

Esplanade
Marine Terrace/Essex Street; tel: 08-9432 4000, toll-free: 1800-998 201; www.esplanadehotel fremantle.com.au; $$$$; train: Fremantle

Elegant gold rush-era building with atrium, two pools, three spas, fitness centre, bar and two restaurants. Most rooms have private balconies with views overlooking popular parklands, tropical gardens and pools. Across Marine Terrace lawns is Fishing Boat Harbour, with restaurants and entertainment venues.

Freo Mews
111 South Terrace; tel: 0415 986 016; www.freomews.com; $$; train: Fremantle

Elegant apartments for up to six people in two-storey mews houses. Comfortable, with good amenities and

Left: relaxing in the pool at the Hyatt Hotel.

Price categories are for a standard double room per night without breakfast.
$$$$ = A$250 plus
$$$ = A$175–$250
$$ = A$100–$175
$ = under A$100

centrally located for all Fremantle attractions.

Pier 21 Resort
7–9 John Street; tel: 08-9336 2555; www.pier21resort. com.au; $$; train: North Fremantle

On the banks of the Swan, fully serviced one- and two-bed apartments with kitchens and river views. Indoor and outdoor pools overlook the river marina; there are also two spas, tennis and squash courts and a barbecue area.

Port Mill
3/17 Essex Street; tel: 08-9433 3832; www.portmillbb.com.au; $$; train: Fremantle

Heritage building in the heart of Fremantle, decorated in modern French style with a Freo twist. Three luxury rooms with wrought-iron balconies overlooking a gorgeous courtyard are available for a romantic experience.

Cottesloe, Claremont, Swanbourne and Scarborough

Cottesloe Beach Chalets
6 John Street, Cottesloe; tel: 08-9383 5000; www.cottesloe beachchalets.com.au; $$; train: Cottesloe

Just off the oceanfront Marine Parade, these self-contained chalets sleep up to five people, with full cooking facilities and laundry available. There is also an on-site pool and barbecue. The nearby pub is a favourite with younger patrons.

The Dunes
15 Filburn Street, Scarborough; tel: 08-9245 2797; www.perth dunes.com; $$; bus: 400

Set back from the West Coast Highway in Scarborough, but close to the beach and local facilities. Modern, well-appointed two-bed units with full kitchens and laundry; there is also a private courtyard with barbecue facilities.

Hillary's Harbour Resort Apartments
68 Southside Drive, Hillary's Boat Harbour; tel: 08-9262 7888, toll-free: 1800-240 078; www.hillarysresort.com.au; $$; train: Warwick, then taxi

Harbour-side one-, two- and three-bedroom modern units on Sorrento Quay boardwalk, with views across the marina; all come with a full kitchen and laundry. There is also a pool, spa and sauna and barbecue area.

Mosman Beach Apartments
3 Fairlight Street, Mosman Park; tel: 08-9285 6400; www. mosmanbeach.com; $$; train: Mosman Park

71

Between Perth and Fremantle, this range of apartments lie just 300m/yds from the beach and are located in a tropical garden setting. There is a heated pool, barbecue area and gym. Great for family groups who aren't too fussy and want to be close to the ocean at a reasonable price.

Ocean Beach Hotel
Eric Street/Marine Parade, Cottesloe; tel: 08-9384 2555; www.obh.com.au; $$; train: Cottesloe
Overlooking the Indian Ocean, this place is right on the beach and ideal for those who want to chill out on the sand and do some surfing. Recently refurbished, it is modern and lively, with a seafront restaurant, café, pizza-bar and two bars heavily used by younger clientele.

Price categories are for a standard double room per night without breakfast.
$$$$ = A$250 plus
$$$ = A$175–$250
$$ = A$100–$175
$ = under A$100

Rendezvous Observation City Hotel
The Esplanade, Scarborough; tel: 08-9245 1000; www.rendezvoushotels.com; $$$; bus: 400
Luxury hotel on the beach, a rare example here of a high-rise building on the coast. Wide-ranging facilities include several restaurants and bars, nightclub, pool, spa, tennis courts and gym. The rooms have been refurbished, but the pool area is still sporting 1980s-style fake rocks and waterfalls.

Sorrento Beach Resort
1 Padbury Circle, Sorrento; tel: 08-9246 8100, toll-free: 1800-998 484; www.sorrentobeach.com.au; $$; train: Warwick, then taxi
Metres from the beach in Sorrento and facing Hillary's Boat Harbour, so handy for the local restaurants, bars, shops, ferry to Rottnest and the AQWA aquarium experience. The resort has an outdoor pool, spa, sauna and barbecue. Hotel-style studio apartments have two or three beds with kitchens.

Sunmoon Resort
200 West Coast Highway, Scarborough; tel: 08-9245 8000; www.sunmoon.com.au; $$; bus: 400
Close to the beach, restaurants and entertainment. Hotel rooms, studio apartments and two- or three-bed units decorated in a distinctly Asian style. Tropical gardens with a pool, and Café Eclipse, a restaurant serving Australasian cuisine.

Swan Valley and the Perth Hills

Carmelot Bed and Breakfast
145 Carmel Road, Carmel; tel: 08-9293 5150; www.camelot.com.au; $; by car
A sense of humour pervades this B&B, with three medieval-themed rooms: King Arthur, Lancelot and Guinevere (with a four-poster, canopied bed). There is a sword set in a stone in the gardens of Carmelot, which is surrounded by

Right: Hillary's Boat Harbour, a good area to stay in when travelling with children.

Left: the Rendezvous Observation City Hotel at Scarborough.

orchards and just five minutes from Kalamunda History Village. Also has a swimming pool, spa and barbecue. All rooms are en suite, and the tariff includes a full cooked breakfast, afternoon tea and a newspaper.

Hidden Valley Eco Retreat
85 Carinyah Road, Pickering Brook; tel: 08-9293 7337; www.hiddenvalleyeco.com; by car

A de luxe spa retreat in the Perth Hills, 45-minutes from the CBD. A range of spa packages is available. There's an outdoor jacuzzi set amongst the jarrah forest and five well-appointed private lodges with forest views. Day visits to the spa also welcomed (daily 9am–6pm).

The Loose Box
6825 Great Eastern Highway, Mundaring; tel: 08-9295 1787; www.loosebox.com.au; $$$$; by car

This fabulous French restaurant also has its own boutique cottages on the property. The idea is that you eat at the restaurant and then stay overnight, and some packages include a dégustation meal in the price.

Novotel Vines Resort
Verdelho Drive, Upper Swan; tel: 08-9297 3000; www.novotelvines.com.au; $$$; by car

Luxury resort and country club noted for its 36-hole championship golf course. Accommodation includes rooms with two double beds, suites with lounges, or self-contained two- or three-bedroom apartments. Restaurants and bars, pool, spa, gym, tennis and squash courts on site.

Possum Creek Lodge
6 Lenori Road, Gooseberry Hill, tel: 08-9257 1927; www.possumcreeklodge.com; $$$; by car

A darling B&B set in a manicured cottage garden. All self-contained, the accommodation ranges from apartments within the homestead

At the time of writing, Perth Airport is undergoing a massive renovation and expansion programme. New regional, domestic and international facilities are being built and a new airport hotel is also part of the plan. This will help with hotel capacity in Perth, especially for passengers in transit.

to two cottages set in the garden. They're warm, cosy and come with generous breakfast provisions – in fact, everything a B&B should be.

Swan Valley Oasis Resort
10250 West Swan Road; tel: 08-9296 5500; www.swanvalleyoasis.com; $$; by car

Set in tropical gardens on 22 hectares (55 acres) by the Swan River, with spa rooms. A luxury self-contained double apartment with kitchen and laundry is also available. The resort has a heated pool and spa, gym, sauna and laundry, and a fully licensed restaurant. You can also play Supa Golf here, with oversized clubs and balls.

Literature

Western Australia is no stranger to the creative arts, and many say that the city's isolation is responsible for its thriving writing scene. Perth and Western Australia can be proud of their literary culture, with several important Australian authors, such as Elizabeth Jolley and Tim Winton, who have immortalised the local life and landscapes in the national consciousness. There are a number of good bookshops here, too, in particular some interesting places to pick up second-hand tomes. Book clubs are popular, too; you will be met with surprise if you can't lay claim to be currently reading something.

Authors

Elizabeth Jolley

Jolley (1923–2007) was born in England and raised in a German-speaking household, but immigrated to WA in 1959, and Perth is happy to claim her as its own. It wasn't until she was in her fifties that she received literary acclaim, but she subsequently won Melbourne's *The Age* newspaper 'Book of the Year' award three times (for *Mr Scobie's Riddle, My Father's Moon* and *The Georges' Wife*), as well as the Miles Franklin prize for *The Well*, while her nonfiction title *Central Mischief* was awarded the WA Premier's Prize in 1993.

Tim Winton

Winton (1960–) was born in WA and still lives here today. He is considered one of Australia's top contemporary authors and began one of his classic titles, *An Open Swimmer,* when he was 19. The book went on to win the Australian/Vogel National Literary Award. Tim is a prolific writer, with many of his novels set in the landscapes of

Above: author Elizabeth Jolley.

WA. He has also written teenage fiction. *Lockie Leonard, Human Torpedo* won the WA Premier's Award for children's fiction and has been adapted into a stage play. Tim has been named a Living Treasure by the National Trust, and awarded the Centenary Medal for service to literature and the community.

Other Significant Authors

Kim Scott was the first Indigenous writer to win the Miles Franklin Literary Award (*Benang*, 2000). Sally Morgan's book *My Place* is an Australian classic. A.B.

Facey's autobiographical work, *A Fortunate Life*, has given voice to the early days of Australia, and T.A.G. Hungerford's collection of autobiographical stories in *Straight Shooter* has become a classic voice of Australian character. English-born author and comedian, Ben Elton, has written more than a dozen novels (*Stark* and *Dead Famous* among them) and today lives in the Fremantle area.

Bookshops

Boffins

806 Hay Street; tel: 08-9321 5755; www.boffinsbookshop. com.au; Mon–Thur 9am– 5.30pm, Fri until 8pm, Sat 9am–5pm, Sun noon–5pm; train: Perth; map p.134 A2 Excellent bookshop specialising in technical and specialist books across all subjects.

Bookcaffe

137 Claremont Crescent, Swanbourne; tel: 08-9385 0553; www.bookcaffe.com.au; Mon–Fri 8.30am–5pm, Sat–Sun 9am–5pm; train: Swanbourne Relax with a coffee and peruse the latest titles.

Left: enticing displays at Elizabeth's Secondhand Bookshop.

Oxford Street Books

119 Oxford Street, Leederville; tel: 08-9443 9844; daily 10am–late; train: Leederville

A small, quirky bookstore with lots of travel, photography, women's studies and children's books. Good selection of fiction, too.

Planet Books

642–48 Beaufort Street, Mount Lawley; tel: 08-9328 7464; www.planetvideo.com.au; daily 10am–10pm; bus: 21, 60; map p.134 B4

Next to the immensely popular Planet Video (which rents videos but also sells a huge range of music, scripts, concert tickets and more), is Planet Books, which stocks a quirky range of texts, from humorous cultural observational scripts to cook books, health texts and more. You are encouraged to browse, and sit and read before buying. The staff is friendly, and the large chandelier in the store sets the mood for fun. You can also buy small gifts such as magnets and cards.

As part of the **Perth International Arts Festival** *(see p.54)*, the Perth Writers Festival happens over three days in February. The festival includes visiting authors, workshops, debate and much more.

Elizabeth's Secondhand Bookshop

820 Hay Street, Perth; tel: 08-9481 8848; www.elizabeths bookshop.com.au; Mon–Thur 9am–5.30pm, Fri until 8pm, Sat until 5pm, Sun 11am–5pm; train: Perth; map p.134 A2

This chain of second-hand bookshops started in the early 1970s, and stocks a large range of all types of literature, from fiction to self-help, coffee-table and children's books and magazines. Books are reasonably priced, but vary in quality. A credit system operates whereby if you take in books to sell you receive a credit amount to spend at the store. When you have read the books, you can return them for more credit. New books are now also sold here. (Additional stores in Fremantle and Subiaco; see the website for details.)

New Edition

82 High Street, Fremantle; tel: 08-9335 2383; www.new edition.com.au; Mon–Fri 7.30am–6pm, Sat 8am–6pm, Sun 9am–6pm; train: Fremantle

A great bookshop with good coffee-table books at the front of the store, lots of political science and a good children's section. Always busy, and you are welcome to sit down and browse.

Reading list

A Fortunate Life, A.B. Facey (UWA Press)
Cloudstreet, Tim Winton (Penguin, Australia)
Dirt Music, Tim Winton (Picador)
My Place, Sally Morgan (Fremantle Press)

Local publishers include Fremantle Press, which was established in 1976, with the aim of developing the widest possible audience for outstanding Western Australian writers and artists. Also prolific in publishing local titles is the University of Western Australia Press.

Below: a fun place to visit for buying books and more.

Museums and Galleries

Spend some time discovering the cultural and historical side of Perth and Western Australia. The Cultural Centre between the CBD and Northbridge is the natural first stop, but Fremantle also offers some fascinating clues into the area's maritime history. From the intriguing and large Aboriginal art collection at the Art Gallery of Western Australia, to the blue whale skeleton at the WA Museum, you will find many exhibits offering different ways to connect to this unusual land.

City Centre

Art Gallery of Western Australia

47 James Street, Perth Cultural Centre; tel: 08-9492 6600; www.artgallery.wa.gov.au; Wed–Mon 10am–5pm; free (temporary exhibitions may charge admission); train: Perth; map p.134 B3

Several floors of modern, well-lit galleries display more than 1,000 works of art, including Australian and international paintings, sculpture, prints, crafts and decorative arts. On the first floor of the main building, two galleries house one of the continent's best collections of Aboriginal art *(see also p.27)*. Also part of the Art Gallery of WA and worth seeing are the **Centenary Galleries**, contained in the former Perth Police Court building. Ask at the front desk to be shown the short cut through to the galleries. Among the highlights here are several paintings from the important Heidelberg School of artists: *Down on His Luck* by Fred McCubbin, *Breaking the News* by John Longstaff, *Ada Furlong* by Tom Roberts, *Black Thursday* by William Strutt and *Hillside* by Arthur Streeton.

Almost as intriguing as the art is the building itself, a late 19th-century interpretation of French Renaissance style. It was unusual for Perth architecture, but localised in its use of WA materials like the pink Donnybrook stone of the facades, hard jarrah timber for floors and interior furnishings, stained-glass feature panels and Australian-made ornate

Below: Gerhard Marks's *The Caller (left)* stands in the grounds of the Art Gallery of WA *(right).*

Left: the International Gallery at the Art Gallery of WA.

mineralogy, meteoritics, anthropology and archaeology, history, maritime history, maritime archaeology and conservation. As some of the oldest land on earth is found in WA, scientists have access to its earliest life forms, and a wealth of artefacts of early man, such as the rock paintings in the Pilbara.

In 1999 a fossil proving the earliest evidence of life on earth was discovered in WA's Pilbara region. Now on display in the Dinosaur Gallery, it looks like a slab of red rock. It holds the oldest life-fossil known, stromatolites estimated to be 3.5 billion years old. Living versions still grow in the highly saline water of Hamelin Pool at Shark Bay, far north of WA.

Australia began taking on its present-day form 120 million years ago, when the supercontinent Gondwana

pressed-metal ceilings. The courts closed in 1982. One courtroom and two adjoining cells are preserved.

There are regular, free public tours of the gallery (Tue–Fri, Sun 1pm, plus a special one focusing on a specific work at 12.30pm on Fri). One painting that is almost always included on the general tour is *The Foundation of Perth*, by George Pitt, depicting the moment when Mrs Dance marked the founding of Perth by attacking a tree with an axe.

The gallery has free Wi-fi, a gallery café overlooking the pedestrian mall, and a calendar of visiting exhibitions that is truly world-class.

Perth Institute of Contemporary Art (PICA) 51 James Street, Perth Cultural Centre; tel: 08-9228 6300; www.pica.org.au; Mon–Fri 10am–6pm, gallery Tue–Sun 11am–6pm; free; train: Perth; map p.134 B3

The PICA building was a school once upon a time, but is now home to Perth's main contemporary art spaces. The soaring main gallery has

studios on a mezzanine, and there's a bar and café and a performance theatre on the ground floor. Sharing space with the Performing Arts Centre Society **(PACS)** are the **Photographers Gallery**, **WA Actors Centre** and **Impressions Gallery**, which exhibits prints. **Artrage**, Perth's alternative arts coordinator, is around the corner. There is usually some contemporary art on show at PICA – photography, installations, large-scale graphic work and audiovisual media are just some of what you can expect.

Western Australian Museum James Street, Perth Cultural Centre; tel: 08-9212 3700; www.museum.wa.gov.au; daily 9.30am–5pm; free; train: Perth; map p.134 B3

Set in an elegant red-brick and sandstone building with a colonnaded upper floor, the collections and research at the WA Museum are centred on systematics, ecology, biogeography, as well as the evolution of living and fossil organisms, palaeontology,

---

One of Western Australia's oldest and wealthiest families are the Holmes à Courts, and they certainly own an impressive art collection. If you are in Margaret River, visit Vasse Felix winery (which the family owns), where you'll not only find modern sculpture in the gardens, but a large Aboriginal art collection inside. In Perth you can visit the Holmes à Court Gallery at level 1, 11 Brown Street in East Perth. The gallery is the passion of Janet Holmes à Court, and its aim is to present exhibitions that 'examine the diversity and strengths of the Holmes à Court Collection'. The collection is impressive and worth a look if you are in the area. See www.holmesacourtgallery.com.au.

complete 1917 pharmacy, clothes, toys and furniture.

Fremantle

Fremantle Arts Centre

1 Finnerty Street; tel: 08-9432 9555; www.fac.org.au; daily 10am–5pm; free; train: Fremantle then the free Fremantle CAT bus from the train station

The former asylum building is one of Fremantle's most significant landmarks. It now houses the Fremantle Arts Centre – a vibrant hub for art, music, education and design. Its exhibitions are often contemporary and cutting edge, and feature local, national and international artists. The café alone is worth a visit. It serves unusual Middle Eastern-inspired breakfasts, yummy lunches, and occasionally holds tapas nights. The retail store is bursting with unusual and 'artsy' gift ideas.

Maritime Museum

Victoria Quay; tel: 08-9431 8444; www.museum.wa.gov.au/maritime; daily 9.30am–5pm; admission charge; train: Fremantle

Fremantle has been the setting for key phases in Western Australia's history, many of them connected with the sea, making it a fitting setting for the Maritime Museum, which opened on Victoria Quay, on the edge of the Indian Ocean, in 2002. Just a few hundred metres along the waterfront is Arthur Head, where Captain Fremantle planted the Union flag and claimed WA for Britain in 1829. The safe anchorage made the colony essential to naval traffic and trade for more than a century, and it was the first sight of Australia

began to break up, separating South America, Africa, Madagascar and India from

Australia. South America was connected to Australia at its southern tip, via an ice-free Antarctica, until 30 million years ago.

Isolated since then, Australia's prehistoric life forms were undisturbed and safe from man until perhaps 50,000–40,000BC. Botanists believe Australia was the prime location of early flowering-plant evolution. Some of the weird and wonderful products of isolation survive, such as the duck-billed platypus, kangaroo and wallaby.

The museum has a pleasant coffee shop next to the Old Gaol, built by convicts in 1855–6 and now crammed with memorabilia of Perth life since James Stirling's expedition of 1827, including a complete original courtroom, a pedal radio that kept outback families in touch, a

While not technically a museum, a visit to the historic Fremantle Prison is a must for history buffs as it's one of the state's most important, and eeriest, heritage sites. Opened to the public in 1992 after 136 years of use, it has housed and hung many of Australia's most infamous criminals. A selection of tours depart hourly throughout the day, but for a truly creepy experience pop on a hard hat and descend 20m/yds into the disturbing darkness for a two-and-a-half-hour tour through the building's labyrinth-like network of secret tunnels (1 The Terrace, Fremantle; tel: 08-9336 9200; www.fremantlepri son.com.au; daily 9am–5pm, admission charge).

for thousands of hopeful migrants until well into the 20th century. Wartime service turned the port into the biggest Allied submarine base outside Pearl Harbor.

The museum covers everything from whaling, pearling, fishing and trade to immigration, recreation and globalisation. There are many delightful details to be discovered along the way, such as the importation of the Mediterranean 'blessing of the sea' festival, introduced to WA by Sicilian fishermen. A highlight is *Australia II*, Australia's historic America's Cup-winning yacht, which now takes pride of place in the museum foyer.

Here you can also tour a decommissioned submarine, HMAS *Ovens*. There is a joint ticket for the museum and a submarine tour, or you can just take the submarine tour. Ticket sales are from the Maritime Museum, with tours running throughout the day.

Moores Building
46 Henry Street, Fremantle; tel: 08-9335 3519; www.fac.org.au/ moores-building; daily 10am– 4pm (café open from 8am); train: Fremantle

Run by the Fremantle Arts Centre, the Moores Building is subsidised by the City of Fremantle and is a vibrant art facility that promotes a wide range of contemporary art by providing artists with a low-cost gallery and project space. Here you'll often find well-priced artwork by little known artists – who knows, you may just find the next big thing before it gets big. The

café at the back of the building is considered one of the best in Fremantle.
SEE ALSO CAFÉS, P.35

Shipwreck Galleries
Cliff Street; tel: 08-9431 8444; www.museum.wa.gov.au/ shipwrecks; daily 9.30am–5pm; free but donations welcome, admission charge for special exhibits may apply; train: Fremantle

Considered the foremost maritime archaeology museum in the southern hemisphere, the Shipwreck Galleries' star exhibit is the stern of the *Batavia*, a Dutch ship wrecked off the Abrolhos islands in 1629, with a famous history. Part of a Dutch expedition to the East Indies, it became separated from its companion

ships on 4 June 1629, when it struck a reef. The crew escaped to two small islands, with provisions and treasure, but little water. While the captain, François Pelsart, and a few other men set off to find help, the ship's officer Jerome Cornelisz mutinied, leading to a bloodbath among the remaining crew.

In September, Pelsart returned. The mutineers were put to death, apart from two, who were marooned near Champion Bay to become the first-known white inhabitants of the continent. Nothing was heard of them again.

The *Batavia* was raised from the depths by marine archaeologists between 1972 and 1976.

Right: HMAS *Ovens* submarine *(top)* and the *Parry Endeavour* yacht *(bottom)* in which Jon Sanders sailed solo around the world in the 1980s, on display at the Maritime Museum.

79

Music
and Dance

Music is a large part of Perth's social scene, and crowds turn out in their thousands for open-air concerts in the summer. Today, Perth is a more popular tour stop than it used to be, and artists such as Elton John, Kanye West and Rod Stewart have recently come to town. Meanwhile, national classical symphony orchestras frequently visit Perth, including the Australian Chamber Orchestra and the Australian String Quartet. For further listings of venues, see *Nightlife, p.85*, and *Pubs and Bars, p.96–9*.

Music

CLASSICAL

His Majesty's Theatre
825 Hay Street; tel: tel: 08-9265 0900; www.hismajestys theatre.com.au; train: Perth; map p.134 A2

A beautiful, ornate Victorian theatre used for all types of concerts, theatre and stand-up comedy.

Perth Concert Hall
5 St George's Terrace; tel: 08-9231 9900; www.perthconcert hall.com.au; train: Perth; map p.134 B1

Perth's principal classical music auditorium is home to the Western Australian Symphony Orchestra (WASO). The Concert Hall also has a huge pipe organ behind the stage, forming a significant part of the rear wall.

West Australian Opera
Concerts are held at various locations; tel: 08-9278 8999; www.waopera.asn.au; bookings tel: 08-9484 1144; www.bocticketing.com.au

The West Australian Opera company enjoys a strong fol-lowing and a talented cast. Classic productions such as *Aida*, *The Barber of Seville* and *The Magic Flute* keep audiences enthralled. The company also has a young artists' programme, where they identify key young performers and run a series of short concerts to show their abilities.

Western Australian Symphony Orchestra
445 Hay Street; tel: 08-9326 0000; www.waso.com.au; train: Perth; map p.134 B2

In 2009, WASO appointed Paul Daniel as its principal conductor. Daniel was music director at the English National Opera from 1997 to 2005 and has guest conducted with major orchestras around the world, including the London Philharmonic, Philharmonia, the Royal Philharmonic, the New York Philharmonic and many orchestras throughout Europe. The WASO's pro-

Right: the ornate facade of His Majesty's Theatre.

Left: Perth has a thriving live music scene.

The Navy Club

64 High Street, Fremantle; tel: 08-9384 8350; www.jazz fremantle.com.au; Sun 4–7pm; admission charge; train: Fremantle

Jazz Fremantle meets at The Navy Club every Sunday. Traditional and mainstream jazz.

Perth Jazz Society

509 Charles Street, North Perth; tel: 08-9444 1051; www.perth jazzsociety.com; admission charge; bus: 400

Held at the Charles Hotel on Monday nights from 8pm, Perth Jazz Society presents a range of excellent artists, both local and international. Founded in 1973, it is a not-for-profit association.

Universal Bar

221 William Street, Northbridge; tel: 08-9227 6771; www.universalbar.com.au; daily noon–late; free; train: Perth; map p.134 A3

Inspired by New Orleans-style jazz and blues bars, the Universal has been a great place to catch live music for almost 20 years.

gramme is always wide and varied, and recently the orchestra has started to venture into some contemporary pairings when visiting musicians call in to Perth. These concerts often take place in Kings Park or Sandalford Winery during summer.

JAZZ

Perth has nurtured an outstanding line-up of talented local jazz musicians, and the pool spreads every year because of the internationally respected Conservatorium at **West Australian Academy of Performing Arts (WAAPA)**. Graduates form many of the groups playing in venues across Perth. Also, Australian and international musicians make regular visits to the west, often at the invitation of the **Perth Jazz Society (PJS)**. Lucky Oceans and Rick Steele are Perth's biggest jazz exports.

The Ellington Jazz Club

191 Beaufort Street, Perth; tel: 08-9228 1088; www.ellingtonjazz.com.au; daily until late; train: Perth; bus: 22; map p.134 B3

This New York-style jazz bar has two spaces – a downstairs cabaret-style space for live performances and an upstairs cocktail lounge. Patrons book tables, from which they enjoy seriously world-class performances while being served their food and drinks. It's a must for lovers of sophisticated jazz.

The Jazz Cellar

Cnr Scarborough Beach and Buxton roads, Mount Hawthorn; tel: 08-9447 8111; www.all aboutjazz.com; Fri 7pm; admission charge; bus: 15

Go through the quirky entrance, a red phone box, and down the stairs for the most intimate of jazz venues; Fri night only. You can BYO food and drinks.

> On its website, the **Perth Jazz Society** has a complete rundown of current venues hosting live jazz in the city. It also runs its own extensive programme of concerts at various pubs, clubs and theatres around town. Visit **www.perthjazzsociety.com** for all things jazz in Perth.

Below: jazz is performed in many types of venues; here, at Friends Restaurant *(see p.102)*.

Left: West Australian Ballet dancers rehearse for the production of *Obsession* at His Majesty's Theatre.

Kulcha
1st floor, 13 South Terrace, Fremantle; tel: 08-9336 4544; www.kulcha.com.au; admission charge; train: Fremantle

Kulcha's focus is on multicultural music and dance, especially world music. Open for classes and specific shows only.

Mustang Bar
46 Lake Street, Northbridge; tel: 08-9328 2350; www.mustang bar.com.au; train: Perth; map p.134 A3

A favourite with the rockabilly set, you can catch some good tunes and jiving here.

The Rosemount Hotel
459 Fitzgerald Street, North Perth; tel: 08-9328 7062; www.rosemounthotel.com.au; admission only on band nights; bus: 19, 400

This is a great spot to catch local rock bands when they're back in town from touring.

MUSIC SHOPS
78 Records
914 Hay Street; tel: 08-9322 6384; Mon–Fri 9am–5.30pm, Sat 9am–5pm, Sun 11am–5pm; train: Perth; map p.133 E2

This store has a huge amount of stock – if you can't find it elsewhere, you're bound to find it here.

Mills Records
22 Adelaide Street, Fremantle; tel: 08-9335 1945; www.mills. com.au; Mon–Thur 9.30am–5.30pm, Fri 9am–7pm, Sat 9am–5pm, Sun noon–5pm; train: Fremantle

A great record store that's jam-packed with great finds – and staffed by people who really know and love their music.

CONTEMPORARY
Western Australia produces even more exponents of rock and pop than jazz; there are live sounds somewhere almost every night. Musically, Perth has always had a thriving local scene with links to some of the most iconic bands in Australian history, such as INXS and AC/DC. AC/DC's original front man Bon Scott, who grew up in Western Australia, is buried in Fremantle Cemetery.

Perth's booming music scene, known in some circles as 'the new Seattle', is largely thanks to the recent success of bands such as Eskimo Joe, The Waifs, John Butler Trio, Little Birdy, Jebediah, the Sleepy Jackson, The Panics, End of Fashion and Gyroscope. To recognise the thriving local industry, there is an annual awards, called the WAMis (West Australian Music Industry), rewarding talents in the industry. These awards are promoted nationally through Triple J Radio (http://triplej.abc.net.au, 99.3FM in Perth).

Fly by Night
Musicians Club
1 Holdsworth Street (entry off Parry Street), Fremantle; tel: 08-9430 5976; www.flybynight.org; admission charge; train: Fremantle

The Fly by Night Musicians Club is a not-for-profit community musicians' club and music venue and probably Perth's most serious music venue. Some of WA's biggest bands, including the John Butler Trio, The Waifs, Eskimo Joe and The Panics, started off their careers here. Worth checking out.

Left: browsing records at one of Perth's stores.

Gilkison Dance Studio
45 Murray Street; tel: 08-9325 6566; www.gilkisons.com.au; train: Perth; map p.134 B2
If you've got some time in Perth, enrol for a series of classes at Gilkison's. Lessons include cha-cha, waltz, jive, tango, samba and more.

The Irish Club
61 Townshend Road, Subiaco; tel: 08-9381 5213; www.irish clubofwa.com.au; train: Subiaco; map p.132 B3
Irish music lessons and set dancing from 8pm, Mondays.

STEPS Youth Dance Company
Level 1, King Street Arts Centre, 357–65 Murray Street; tel: 08-9226 2133; www.stepsyouth dance.com.au; train: Perth; map p.134 A2
Another youth dance group, STEPS was founded in 1988 and has a focus on dance relevant to young people, and to assisting young dancers in working together and in performance. Only the cream of Perth's young talent is invited to join the company.

Urban Records
117 Oxford Street, Leederville; tel: 08-9201 2500; daily 10am–late; train: Leederville
This record store has a good mix of contemporary music, from club to rock to world. Walk through, and at the rear you will find a quirky shop selling clothing and gifts.

Dance
CLASSICAL
West Australian Ballet
134 Whatley Crescent, Maylands; tel: 08-9214 0707; www.waballet.com.au; train: Maylands

Madame Bousloff, who founded West Australian Ballet, was a prima ballerina with the Ballets Russes and travelled to the east coast of Australia in 1938. After completing her commitment with the Ballets Russes she travelled west to Perth on holiday and fell in love with the city, declaring that the beautiful coastline reminded her of the French Riviera.

In 1952, Madame Kira Bousloff established the West Australian Ballet, the first ballet company in Australia.

The company stages everything from full-length classical ballets and narrative ballets to shorter works, and encompasses a variety of choreographic styles. West Australian Ballet also tours nationally and internationally, as well as conducting regional tours in Western Australia.

CONTEMPORARY
Buzz Dance Theatre
King Street Arts Centre, 357–65 Murray Street; tel: 08-9226 2322; www.buzzdance.com.au; train: Perth; map p.134 A2
The Buzz Dance Theatre was founded in 1985 and is a leading company for children and young dancers. They are heavily involved at school level, tour nationally and internationally, and come into contact with more than 20,000 youth, teachers, families and communities each year.

Below: West Australian Ballet founder, Madame Bousloff.

Nightlife

If you expect Perth to be up until the wee hours on a Tuesday night, think again. The clubbing scene is very much limited to the weekend, the biggest nights for going out being Saturday and Sunday. In the week, locals are more likely to head out for dinner and a quiet drink at the pub, so if you want to party with your fellow man, it is best to aim for the high-ticket weekend nights, when clubs stay open until 4–5am and most of the population are willing to nurse a hangover the next day. Alternatively, for some evening entertainment mid-week, hit the Crown Casino or one of the comedy nights on offer.

Casino

Crown Casino

Great Eastern Highway, Burswood; tel: 08-9362 7777; daily 24 hours; admission charge; bus: 37

WA's only casino is open 24 hours in Crown Perth (formerly the Burswood Entertainment Complex), with nine restaurants and six bars. There is a dress code of no jeans, vests, thongs (flip-flops) or sneakers, but once you are inside you'll wonder who was in charge of enforcing the dress standards. There is an international room for high rollers only.

Below: in the Crown Casino.

Comedy

Comedy Lounge

The Charles Hotel, 509 Charles Street, North Perth; tel: 1300 LIVE COMEDY; www.comedylounge. com.au; shows: Thur 7pm; admission charge; bus: 19, 346

Comedy Lounge brings local, inter-state and international acts to Perth. There is usually a Thursday night gig which runs for a couple of hours. The company also runs a Saturday evening gig at Little Creatures Loft, Fremantle (tel: 08-9430 5555).

The Laugh Resort

Rosie O'Grady's, Cnr James and Milligan streets, Northbridge; tel: 0421 821 320; www.laughresort.com.au; shows: Wed 8pm; admission charge; train: Perth; map p.134 A3

Every Wednesday night at The Brass Monkey pub, The Laugh Resort is a place to spy local stand-up comedians. There's also a chance to test your own humour, as they offer open mic, too.

Lazy Susan's Comedy Den

Brisbane Hotel, Cnr Brisbane and Beaufort streets, Highgate; tel: 08-9328 2543; bookings through BOCS: 08-9484 1133; www.lazysusans.com.au; shows: Fri 8pm; admission charge; bus: 60; map p.134 B4

Friday night is stand-up night, upstairs at the Brisbane. See the gig guide on the website for other events.

Food

Sadly, late-night food options are scarce in Perth, especially if you want something other than fast food.

Billy Lees

66 Roe Street, Perth; tel: 08-9328 4003; daily until 4am; train: Perth; map p. 134 A3

Located in Northbridge's China Town, Billy Lees isn't fancy, but dishes up good, authentic, cheap Chinese food into the wee hours. It's at its busiest around 2am.

Cosmos Kebabs

129 Oxford Street, Leederville; tel: 08-9444 8429; daily 11am–3am; train: Leederville

If you've been dancing up a storm at one of Leederville's pubs or clubs, then Cosmos is a required pit stop. It specialises in excellent kebabs. Their chips are also first rate, and while the decor is

Left: mid-week cocktails.

With 10 bars offering a diversity of music from R&B to hip-hop and dance, and the capacity for 2,000 people, 'Metros' is Perth's largest super-club. On other nights, it's a popular place for visiting bands to play, plus they often have international DJs.

Metropolis Fremantle
58 South Terrace, Fremantle; tel: 08-9336 1880; www.metropolis fremantle.com.au; Fri–Sat 8pm–late, Sun 8pm–midnight; admission charge; train: Fremantle

Large club divided into four 'chambers', each playing a different style of music. A true stayer on the nightlife scene.

The Red Sea
83 Rokeby Road, Subiaco; tel: 08-9382 2022; Wed 9am–3am; every alternate Thur, and Fri–Sat 9pm–late; admission charge; train: Subiaco; map p.132 B3

A very popular nightclub with two dance floors. Fun, laid-back, and less hardcore than other clubs in town.

Above: the distinctive signage of the Brass Monkey pub.

awful, the service patchy and the old Greek men who invariably are sitting out the front always are surly, this place does well for both its late hours and great food.

Fast Eddys
454 Murray Street; tel: 08-9321 2552; daily 24 hours; train: Perth; map p.133 E3

An American diner-style café, where burgers are big and sloppy but tasty. The fries are chunky and loaded with salt, often what you crave after a night out. There is a large menu, and a takeaway area that does burgers, hot dogs and chips. An institution.

Purl Bar
71–5 Rokeby Road; tel: 08-9381 7755; www.purlbar.com.au; Mon–Fri from noon for lunch, Mon–Sat from 5.30pm for dinner, Fri–Sat 9.30pm–1am; $$; train: Subiaco; map p.132 B3

In the heart of Subi, this brand new, laid-back bar and restaurant offers a weekend late-night menu of Middle-Eastern inspired bites – very unusual for Perth.
SEE ALSO RESTAURANTS, P.105

Nightclubs

The Deen
84 Aberdeen Street, Northbridge; tel: 08-9227 9361; www.thedeen.com.au; Mon, Thur–Sat 7pm–2am; train: Perth; map p.134 A3

With a real party atmosphere The Deen is half pub, half club with nine different bars playing everything from commercial dance to house and traditional party hits.

Metro City
146 Roe Street, Northbridge; tel: 08-9228 0500; www.metro concertclub.com; Thur–Sat 9pm–late, from 8pm for live music; admission charge; train: Perth; map p.134 A3

Taxis are an issue in Perth: there simply aren't enough where and when you need them, especially after midnight at weekends. They may also choose longer trips over shorter ones, so if you call one but don't want to go far, keep calling the taxi company to make sure one is on its way. Note that taxi drivers aren't fond of taking inebriated people home, especially a large group of men. Reliable firms include: **Swan Taxis** (tel: 13 13 30) and **Black and White Taxis** (tel: 13 10 08). Swan Taxis have introduced an app for iPhones and android handsets. Book through the app and you'll be picked up quickly and you can track your taxi's route.

Pampering

With Perth's booming economy there seems to be no shortage of ways to spend money. The spa and beauty scene is thriving, with more and more salons and wellness centres offering treatments for men as well as women. The trend in Perth is to treat spa and beauty treatments as seriously as a haircut, an important part of maintenance and overall well-being. However, even though many local people would like to visit day spas frequently, the treatments are not cheap and sometimes get reserved for special occasions, so do call ahead if you feel like treating yourself to some special Perth pampering.

Beauty Products

Kit Cosmetics

Enex100, St George's Terrace, Perth; tel: 08-9486 7610; www.kit cosmetics.com.au; Mon–Thur 9am–5.30pm, Fri until 9pm, Sat 9am–5pm, Sun 11am–5pm; train: Perth; map p.134 A2

Kit stocks lust-worthy beauty products from around the world and is the younger, funkier sister to Mecca. Both men and women are looked after, and you will always discover something fun and interesting to play with. Staff are friendly and happy to help.

For a spa experience you won't forget, head to **Empire Retreat** (www.empireretreat.com) in Yallingup. A 2½-hour drive south of Perth, Empire is set amongst 105 hectares (264 acres) of bushland, undulating pastures and vineyards. It's a luxury adult-only boutique retreat with a renowned day spa where earthy treatments are offered. The suites are sumptuous and all have an outdoor shower. The perfect place for relaxation and solitude.

(There is a second store inside Myer in the Murray Street Mall, tel: 08-9265 5872.)

Mecca Cosmetica

Claremont Quarter, Bay View Terrace, Claremont; tel: 08-9286 2477; www.mecca cosmetica.com.au; Mon–Fri 9am–5.30pm, Thur until 9pm, Sat 9am–5pm; train: Claremont

If you like the best of the best when it comes to skincare and make-up, Mecca Cosmetica is a must. It stocks perfumes, skin care products, make-up, toothpaste, nail polish and more for both men and women, and you can lose hours poring over the luxurious brands. Staff are well informed about the products; make sure you ask for help, as you will learn much more and be pointed in the right direction. Brands include Nars, Stila, Malin+Goetz, NV Perricone, Philosophy, Kiehl's, Du Wop, Kevyn Aucoin and Bumble and Bumble.

Salons and Spas

Affinity Day Spa

16 Station Street, Cottesloe; tel: 08-9284 4333; www.affinity dayspa.com.au; Mon–Sat

9am–5.30pm, Thur until 9pm, Sat until 5pm; train: Cottesloe

Situated in Cottesloe, one of Perth's most affluent suburbs, this lush day spa offers a wide range of treatments, from packages of facials and massages lasting hours to acrylic nails, body wraps, oxygen face treatments, hydrotherapy and tanning.

Guys Grooming

Shop G5, 160 Central Arcade, 811 Hay Street; tel: 08-9226 3022; www.guysgrooming. com.au; Mon–Fri 8am–6pm; train: Perth; map p.134 A2

Offering a place for guys to go that is definitely a male space, with all grooming needs taken care of. Hair-cuts, traditional face shaves, waxing, massage, facials, manicures and pedicures are all on offer.

Hidden Valley Eco Retreat

85 Carinyah Road, Pickering Brook; tel: 08-9293 7337; www.hiddenvalleyeco.com; daily 9am–6pm (spa); by car

Make a weekend of it and head to this de luxe spa retreat in the Perth Hills, a 45-minute drive from the CBD. In the spa a range of packages from basic mas-

Left: the beauty emporium of Mecca Cosmetica.

bushy, go to see him. It's not cheap, but you'll either receive a free eyebrow gel, mini tweezers or a discount off products purchased.

Spa at the Richardson
The Richardson Hotel, 32 Richardson Street; tel: 08-9217 8888; www.therichardson. com.au/spa; Wed–Sat 9.30am–8.30pm, Sun–Tue 9.30pm–6.30pm; booking required; bus: red CAT; map p.133 D3

This spa is in the boutique Richardson Hotel *(see Hotels, p.66)*, but you don't have to be a guest to have a session here. The spa is Asian-style with dark timbers, soothing music and top treatments including facials, massage and wraps.

sages through to a full day of indulgence are offered. There's an outdoor jacuzzi set on a private deck amongst the jarrah forest. The five private lodges are well appointed and have forest views. Day visits are also welcomed and individual packages can be arranged.
SEE ALSO HOTELS, P.73

Keturah Spa and Skincare
5/500 Beaufort Street, Highgate; tel: 08-9228 0855; www.keturah.com.au; Mon–Sat 9am–5.30pm, Thur until 8.30pm; bus: 67; map p.134 C4
Keturah was one of the pioneers of the beauty scene in Perth and now has a long list of available services, including a list for men. Beyond the usual array of facials and massages, Keturah also do micro-dermabrasion, peels, light treatments, water therapy, and have an infra-red sauna. Other salons can be found in Fremantle, Nedlands and Carine Glades.

Le Beau Day Spa
75 Gilbertson Road, Kardinya; tel: 08-9331 1122; www.day-spa-perth.com; Mon–Sat 9am–5pm; bus: 940

Le Beau is the most awarded day spa in the Perth area, and while externally the location doesn't appear to be that tranquil, once you are through the doors, the outside world disappears. There is a Balinese-style relaxation area, hydrobath, Vichy shower, eight-seater outdoor spa and sauna. Treatments include Indian oil massage, hot stone therapy, waxing, tanning, nails, and facials using Guinot, Gatineau and Thalgo. There is Napoleon Perdis make-up, too. At the end of facials and massages you are given a cleansing fruit platter and juice and left to relax for as long as you like.

Matt Yuko
30/22 St Quentin Avenue, Claremont; tel: 08-9385 2006; www.mattyuko.com.au; Mon–Sat 9am–5pm; train: Claremont
Matt Yuko specialises in eyebrows. And that's it. He's known as 'the eyebrow king' and his fans think he's a genius, so if your brows are

Right: indulge in some relaxation at one of Perth's day spas.

87

Parks

There are numerous parks in the city centre where you can while away some time in the almost perennially pleasant weather. However, if you fancy venturing further afield, there are beautiful national parks located within driving distance of Perth; generally speaking, access to the parks is best by car. When walking in the Western Australian national parks, wear a wide-brimmed hat, sunscreen with a sun protection factor of 30-plus, and sturdy shoes. Take plenty of drinking water with you, at least three litres per day, more if the weather is very hot. In most park areas you will not be able to access clean drinking water.

City Parks

Araluen Botanical Gardens

Croyden Road, off Brookton Highway, Roleystone; tel: 08-9496 1171; www.araluenbotanic park.com.au; daily; admission charge; by car

Araluen is one of Perth's greatest attractions. Bush walks by flowing streams and picnic spots among spectacular garden displays are boosted with mass plantings of bulbs, annuals and other plants from August through to October. Araluen is an eastern states Aboriginal word meaning 'singing waters' or 'place of lilies'. A 'Grove of the Unforgotten' is a tribute to 88 Young Australia League members killed in World War I. Araluen was restored by the government in the 1990s, and new works include a spectacular watercourse.

The Esplanade

Bordered by Barrack Street and Riverside Drive; daily; free; bus: blue CAT; map p.134 A1

The Esplanade overlooks Barrack Square and the Swan River and is essentially just a nice open place, without very many plants, but it's where you will find lots of activity during city lunch breaks. Outdoor exercise classes are held here, and throughout the year sporting events, such as polo matches, and some high profile concerts, are staged in the park.

You will also notice a pyramid-shaped greenhouse. Called the Allan Green Conservatory. It once housed exotic tropical plants and rare palms but is currently closed to the public while the city council resolves its future –

Above: the State War Memorial Cenotaph obelisk in Kings Park.

redeveloping the building to become a restaurant or café is being investigated. Across the park at Barrack Square are the Swan Bells (www. swanbells.com.au; daily from 10am, closing times vary according to season; admission charge); to see the historical bells being rung; check times online. You can climb to the top of the bell tower and the view is certainly worth it. SEE ALSO SWAN RIVER AND KINGS PARK, P.6

Heirisson Island

Near Causeway, end of Riverside Drive; free; train: Perth; map p.139 D3–E4

Left: native gum trees in Kings Park.

The first public park in the city was Queen's Gardens, in East Perth. It was created in 1899 out of clay pits that for 50 years supplied bricks for buildings such as Perth Town Hall. Lily ponds and English trees show the gardens' British influences, as does the 1927 statue of Peter Pan, a replica of the one that stands in London's Kensington Gardens.

The walk from Barrack Street Jetty to Heirisson Island can be done comfortably in 30 minutes. At the end of Riverside Drive follow the path up onto the Causeway, turn right off the Causeway, and follow the track down towards an orange sign, with the river on your right. A small colony of western grey kangaroos are housed in an enclosure here, bringing an iconic bush element right into the city. During the heat of the day kangaroos stay under cover, but if you move quietly around the track there's a good chance of finding them grazing.

There is a 2km (1-mile) track around Heirisson Island. At the southern tip is a bronze statue of Yagan, an Aboriginal leader killed in 1833. The statue has been vandalised on numerous occasions over the years.

The island was named after a French sailor, midshipman François Heirisson. Long before the founding of Perth, he rowed a longboat all the way upriver to the island from his moored ship

Le Naturaliste, which carried Nicolas Baudin's scientific expedition of 1801–4. As late as the 1920s, squatters lived rough in shacks on the island, in sight of Government House. In 1984 an Aboriginal camp lasted for 40 days before its occupants, land-rights protesters, were evicted. In 2012 fresh protests saw land-rights activists illegally camp on the island for over six weeks. The Aboriginal community has recently allowed outdoor concerts to be held here.

Hyde Park

Cnr Vincent, William, Glendower and Throssell streets; Wed–Sat 7am–5pm, Sun 7am–1pm; free; bus: 67; map p.134 B4

Hyde Park is a beautiful space, filled with mature trees. In the centre of the park is a small lake surrounded by weeping willows. There is playground equipment, a water playground, free electric barbecues, drinking fountains and public toilets. It is a meeting point for Aboriginal families, and the path around the lake is well frequented by walkers

and joggers. In the surrounding streets you'll discover beautiful examples of 'federation' and terrace homes. On the nearby Lincoln Street there is a Swiss-French bakery called the Pearl of Highgate, ideal for picking up picnic goodies.

Kings Park

Off Kings Park Road; Park Visitor Information tel: 08-9480 3634; www.bgpa.wa.gov.au; daily 9.30am–4pm; park access daily 24 hours; free; bus: 102, 78, 24, 37; map p.132–3 B1–D2, 136–7 A3–D4

Below: the monument of Queen Victoria in Kings Park.

Kings Park is integral to Perth's identity. There's no other city in the world with as big an area of natural bushland at its centre. Much of the park is rough bushland, with walking paths running throughout. There are beautiful cultivated lawns, terraces and water gardens throughout the park, many positioned to take in sweeping views of the Swan River, thanks to the park's high vantage point over the city and river. The park covers 400 hectares (988 acres), and Park Visitor Information offers free half-day bush and wildflower walks conducted by volunteer guides.

The park is full of war memorials, and Fraser Avenue is no exception. The ranks of magnificent lemon-scented gums, known as the widow-maker's tree on account of its habit of shedding large branches during times of drought, were planted to mark WA's 1929 centenary. Individual gums lining May Avenue and Lovekin Drive commemorate the fallen of two world wars. As well as the Cenotaph, other memorials commemorate victims of the Bali bombing of 2002, Western Australian victims of the South African War of 1899–1902 (just off Fraser Avenue) and victims of the Vietnam War (near Western Power playground).

A memorial to the Australians who fought and died on the Kokoda Trail during the Japanese invasion of Papua New Guinea in World War II is also found nearby. If you stay on the road, rather than the path, you will approach the Cenotaph through the Whispering Wall, which commemorates battles in which Australians have fought. The huge river gum just past here was planted by Elizabeth II in 1954, during one of her Australian tours.

Beyond the Cenotaph are the heavily planted sections of the **Botanic Gardens** (daily 24 hours; free). Any of the paths to the right will lead to exotic plants and trees, including many hundreds of native species.

By keeping to the left-hand path, with the Swan River on your left, you will come to a Tree-Top Walk with views across the river, and then enter an area of native bush (stay on the marked paths), eventually exiting the park on Park Avenue, in an exclusive neighbourhood called Crawley, about 2km (1 mile) west from the University of Western Australia *(see below right)*. Back in the Botanic Gardens, between the riverside path and Forest Drive, is the Pioneer Women's Memorial, a grassy bowl with an ornamental lake and fountain that doubles as an open-air venue in summer.

Close by is the Broadwalk, a grassy swath with a high lookout, known as the DNA tower because of its twin circular staircases; from here you can see Rottnest Island *(see p.46–8)* about 30km (18 miles) away. The Broadwalk leads, after about 2km (1½ miles), to Synergy Parkland and lake. Lycopod Island in the centre of the lake has model dinosaurs and timber-and-steel lycopods (the world's first trees), and

Left: contemplation at the State War Memorial Cenotaph, on the edge of Kings Park.

Above: the Karrakatta Club in Stirling Gardens, the oldest in the city.

calamites (fern-like plants). In the lake, replicas of 3.5 billion-year-old stromatolites are inset with solar cells to power the misty spray.

The Lotterywest Family area, off Kings Park Road, has been extensively refurbished and is ideal for families with children of all ages. There's a café that sells popular snacks and healthy lunches, a playground specifically for children under five, an area designed for older children, as well as Hale Oval with a cricket pitch, acres of shaded picnic lawns and free barbeques.

Below: Government House, in Stirling Gardens.

Stirling Gardens
Cnr St George's Terrace and Barrack Street; daily; free; bus: blue CAT; map p.134 B1

Stirling Gardens, named after Captain James Stirling, who founded Perth, are the oldest gardens in the city. They were started in the 1830s and in 1845 opened as a botanical garden. In 1960, Kings Park Botanic Garden opened, ending the need for Stirling Gardens to be the state's botanic park. At the entrance to the gardens is a statue of Alexander Forrest who was an explorer and early mayor of Perth. Within the gardens you'll also find kangaroo sculptures, a water feature and sculptures of Snugglepot and Cuddlepie, characters from May Gibbs's children's book of the same name. The gardens border Council House, where the Perth Lord Mayor's offices are situated.

Supreme Court Gardens
Cnr Barrack Street and Riverside Drive; daily; free; bus: blue CAT; map p.134 A1–B1

The Supreme Court Gardens (see p.8) merge with Stirling Gardens and are a beautiful, quiet place to while away a break in the city. During the summer, large outdoor concerts are held here, with up to 8,000 people converging on the garden space. At Christmas, this is the location for Carols by Candlelight. There is a large central grassed area fringed with tropical-looking verdant plants, with some park benches on the periphery if you don't feel like lying on the lawn. Across Barrack Street you will find the Esplanade.

UWA was the first free university of the British Commonwealth. Across the Reflecting Pool is Winthrop Hall, with its undercroft terracotta frieze of gryphons and 50m (164ft) clock tower. To the right, across Whitfield Court, the colonnaded building is the original library (now admin offices), and more pillars hold up Hackett Hall, on the left. All were built in 1932 with an endowment from Sir John Winthrop Hackett, the first Chancellor of UWA and also the owner of Perth's daily newspaper, The West Australian. The design was by the Victorian architects Sayce and Alsop, who won an international competition for the commission.

91

University of Western Australia

Winthrop Avenue, Crawley; www.uwa.edu.au; daily; free; bus: 78, 102; map p.136 A2

The grounds of the University of Western Australia are worth taking an amble around. Stop in at the visitor centre (north end of the admin office building) near Winthrop Hall off Winthrop Avenue and ask to be shown where the prettiest areas are: they have booklets and often guided tours are run. The sunken garden is a popular spot to get married in, but there are other places worth a visit, too. Peacocks stroll around the Greek-Revival-style architecture, too.

National Parks

For detailed information on all Western Australian national parks visit the Department of Environment and Conservation website: www.dec.wa.gov.au.

Cape Range

Admission charge; by car

Lying predominantly on the western side of Northwest Cape Peninsula, Cape Range National Park protects an area of 50,581 hectares (126,453 acres). The northern boundary of the park is 39km (24 miles) from Exmouth by road, and the southern boundary is 70km (43 miles) north of Coral Bay.

The time to visit is between April and September, when you'll have the best weather to go for walks, see wildlife, picnic, camp, canoe and explore caves. Nearby Ningaloo Marine Park offers some of the world's best dives, and in season you can dive with majestic whale sharks.

There are a number of camping areas all along the stunning, white sandy coast, from Boat Harbour to Ned's Camp. Entry charges apply. There are also picnic facilities and toilets at many sites. No campfires are allowed in the park: gas barbecues only.

The Cape Range is the only elevated limestone range on the northwestern coast of WA. The impressive weathered limestone range has plateaux of up to 314m (1,030ft) high. It forms the spine of the peninsula that stretches up towards Northwest Cape in the Gascoyne region of Western Australia. You can climb up deep rocky gorges to enjoy breathtaking scenery. One of many popular walks is a 3km (2-mile) ramble through Mandu Mandu Gorge along the bed of an ancient river. As the summer heat is intense, walks should only be attempted between April and September. You can also view rock wallabies at Yardie Creek.

Beneath the rocky plateaux and canyons of the Cape Range National Park lies a network of hidden caves and tunnels. They harbour a unique collection of bizarre cave-dwelling animals: an ancient treasure trove of immense value to both science and nature conservation.

D'Entrecasteaux

Admission charge; by car

The D'Entrecasteaux National Park stretches along the coast for 130km (80 miles) from Black Point (35km/22 miles east of Augusta), to Long Point (10km/6 miles west of Walpole) and extends inland for between 5 and 20km (3–12 miles). It lies 8km (5 miles) from Northcliffe and 40km (25 miles) from Pemberton.

Spectacular coastal cliffs, beaches, mobile sand dunes, vast coastal wild-flower heaths and even pockets of karri are all part of the scenery of D'Entrecasteaux National Park. The park has isolated beach campsites, wild coastal vistas and excellent fishing. Much of the park is managed for its wilderness values, so few facilities are provided.

Major streams and rivers, including the Warren, Donnelly and Shannon, drain through D'Entrecasteaux and empty into its coastal waters. High sand dunes and limestone cliffs on the sea coast give way to coastal heathlands and a series of lakes and swamps further inland. These include Lake Yeagarup and Lake Jasper, which is the largest freshwater lake in the southern half of Western Australia.

Vast areas of wetlands behind the coastal dunes are

Below: typical Western Australian bush terrain.

Above: watch out for emus and kangaroos in the bush: both are fairly common sights.

known as The Blackwater. Another outstanding feature is the Yeagarup Dune, an impressive mobile dune 10km (6 miles) long.

Much of the park is off limits to cars, especially if you don't have a four-wheel-drive vehicle. The basalt columns west of Black Point are one of the park's most stunning landforms. This feature originated from a volcanic lava flow some 135 million years ago. The formation resulted from the slow cooling of a deep pool of lava, similar to the development of mud cracks. In the process of it cracking and shrinking, columns were formed perpendicular to the surface. The result was a close-packed series of hexagonal columns, now slowly being eroded by the sea.

There are several beaches suitable for car access: Windy Harbour, Salmon Beach and Broke Inlet are the only coastal areas of this large park that are accessible by conventional vehicle. Four-wheel-drive tracks lead to other coastal fishing and camping spots. Stay on existing tracks and reduce your tyre pressure in summer to cope with sand.

Sand tracks make travelling slow inside the park. Many places, such as the mouth of the Donnelly River, can be reached only by small boats. Significant vehicle-exclusion areas provide those who are willing to hike with an opportunity to experience seclusion on a deserted beach. If you intend to go walking, make sure you are properly equipped with map, compass, water and sun protection, as this is wild country. There are campsites throughout the park, some charging small camping fees.

John Forrest National Park
Free; by car

John Forrest is one of Australia's oldest conservation areas and Western Australia's first national park. The area was first established in 1898 as a reserve to conserve its natural and cultural features.

It became John Forrest National Park in 1947, named in honour of the famous WA explorer and statesman. Recreation is an important use of the park. It provides magnificent vistas of the Swan coastal plain and contains walking trails through rugged

wilderness, along the old railway line or to quiet pools and spectacular waterfalls.

On the western boundary of the park is the Rocky Pool picnic area, which is set among attractive wandoo and paperbark woodland. Here, after winter rains, you can sit

When driving on country roads, be aware that kangaroos can jump in front of your car, and emus can run onto the road. These animals are most active at dawn and dusk, so take extra care at these times. Kangaroos especially can become stunned by car headlights. If a roo does jump in front of your car, do not attempt to swerve and miss it. The best thing to do is to keep going following the direction of the road, as swerving means you could hit a tree at the side of the road, and probably also still hit a roo. They often travel in groups, so if you see one, there's probably another close behind.

If it seems like a kangaroo might hit your car and come through the windscreen, put your arms up across your face so their scratching claws don't get your face and chest.

93

eral camping areas with some basic facilities.

Yalgorup
Free; by car

Yalgorup National Park lies on the western edge of the Swan Coastal Plain just south of the new Dawesville Channel near Mandurah.

The name Yalgorup is derived from two Noongar Aboriginal words: *Yalgor*, meaning a swamp or lake, and *up*, a suffix meaning a place. In the early 1970s Yalgorup National Park was formally established to protect the coastal lakes, swamps and tuart woodland between Mandurah and Myalup Beach. The park is of significant scientific interest: the dune systems are a result of changes in sea level hundreds of thousands of years ago, right up to the end of the last Ice Age, around 10,000 years ago. The lakes in the park are surrounded with important water-bird

and watch the waters of Jane Brook tumble down a series of small rapids into the pool.

In summer the hills area can get very hot, so the best times to visit are in autumn, winter and spring, when you can enjoy a relaxing picnic or bush stroll.

Leeuwin-Naturaliste
Free; by car

Leeuwin-Naturaliste National Park stretches 120km (75 miles) from Bunker Bay in the north to Augusta in the south of the Margaret River region. Most roads in the area are sealed. Gravel roads are usually suitable for two-wheel-drive vehicles.

Between Cowaramup Bay and Karridale, the Leeuwin-Naturaliste National Park features some of its most rugged and inaccessible coastline. Facing due west, the coastal cliffs and rocky shoreline bear the brunt of giant ocean swells generated across thousands of miles of ocean by

the prevailing westerly and southwesterly winds. Scenic lookouts from which to marvel at the ocean's beauty and power are found at intervals along the coast.

You might be lucky enough to see humpback and southern right whales from various vantage points along the coast, and bushwalking attracts people right into the heart of the park.

There are several short walks and trails through this area, and the beach scenery is spectacular. The Cape to Cape Walk track runs 140km (87 miles) from Cape Naturaliste to Cape Leeuwin, but you can break it down into smaller sections. Brochures on walking trails are available at Cape Naturaliste, Yallingup, Margaret River and the Cape to Cape Walk. There are sev-

Koalas are not native to Western Australia, and you'll rarely see them in the wild. They can be aggressive, and do not conform to the 'cuddly' image many people have of them. Never approach any native animal in the wild; most won't let you get anywhere near them, but it is best not to try.

Above: a koala dozes in Yanchep National Park.

habitat, but more interestingly, rock-like structures called thrombalites can be found on the edge of Lake Clifton. While they look like rocks, thromblates are alive, built by micro-organisms. These organisms were the only known form of life on Earth from 3,500 million to 650 million years ago.

Today, living examples of these once completely dominant organisms are restricted to only a few places. So why do thrombolites grow at Yalgorup? Scientists have suggested it is perhaps because Lake Clifton is associated with upwellings of fresh groundwater that are high in calcium carbonate. The micro-organisms living in this shallow lake environment are able to precipitate calcium carbonate from the waters as they photosynthesise, forming the mineralised structure that is the thrombolite.

The significance of thrombolites and stromatolites to science is inestimable, but they are very fragile and can be degraded by visitors walking over them. To protect the thrombolites, an observation walkway has been built to minimise any impact from visitors wanting to see these fascinating structures.

Yanchep National Park
Free; by car

Only 51km (32 miles) north of Perth, reaching this park will only require a 45-minute drive. Just follow Wanneroo Road north about 25km (16 miles) past Wanneroo and you will see the Yanchep National Park signs. Known as Perth's natural and cultural meeting place, the park is home to many native birds and lots of kangaroos.

The National Park environment provides a unique setting to experience environmental and cultural activities that are informative and promote awareness about natural areas. Several of the caves in Yanchep National Park have been open for tourists during the past 70 years or so. These include Cabaret, Mambibby, Yanchep, Yonderup and Crystal caves. There have been more than 600 caves documented in the park.

There are self-guided walks here, plus a boardwalk that has been built in order for visitors to enjoy watching the koalas that live in the park.

95

Pubs and Bars

A s in the rest of the country, going to the pub is a popular pastime of West Australians, and many establishments offer good menus alongside the beer. Legislation changes in Perth in 2008 meant that smaller bars seating up to 80 people could more easily come into existence, with the hope that Perth would develop more of the quirky, small-bar culture that Melbourne has, and fewer of the barn-style pubs that have existed for so long. The plan is working – today a host of small bars and bistros litter Perth's inner city lanes and are springing up in suburban areas, much to the delight of locals.

Swan River and Kings Park

Amphoras
1303 Hay Street; tel: 08-9226 4666; www.amphorasbar. com.au; Mon–Fri 9am–late, Sat 4pm–late; bus: red CAT; map p.133 D3
This new bar offers a good wine list, which errs on the fancier, pricier side, and a concise but solid tapas menu. Packed out on Friday nights, it has a great vibe.

The Lucky Shag Waterfront Bar
Barrack Street Jetty; tel: 08-9221 6011; www.theluckyshag barcom.au; daily 11am–late; bus: blue CAT; map p.134 A1
This popular pub overlooks the river, with a good range

of beers and wines, plus live music and DJs at weekends. Food is available, too. In case you're wondering, shags are sea birds and they are often seen perched by the water drying their wings.

City Centre

Andaluz
Basement Level, 21 Howard Street, tel: 08-9481 0092; www.andaluzbar.com.au; Mon–Fri noon–late, Sat 6pm–late; bus: red CAT; map p.134 A2
With Chesterfield couches, mood lighting and an elegant courtyard, Andaluz is a glamorous, den-like space that's popular with the nine-to-five crowd. Its maze of intimate rooms gets packed to the

Where bars are said to stay open 'late', which means between 2 and 4am (although sometimes they will remain open until 6am in the summer).

rafters and its tapas menu is one of the most authentic in Perth. Arrive early.

Helvetica
Rear 101 St George's Terrace; tel: 08-9321 4422; www.helveticabar.com.au; Tue–Thur 3pm–late, Fri noon–late, Sat 6pm–late; bus: red CAT; map p.134 A2
Hidden among office buildings on St George's Terrace is this moody little treasure – top-shelf whisky, classy cocktails and good bar snacks.

Venn
16 Queen Street, Perth; tel: 08-9321 8366; www.venn.net; Mon–Tue 7am–5pm, Wed–Fri 7am–midnight, Sat 9am–midnight; train: Perth; bus: red CAT; map p. 134 A2
Relaxed and intimate, this popular café/bar is one of the hippest addresses in town. The uber-cool space sits

Left: the Lucky Shag.

Left: a trip to the bar at The Brass Monkey.

0466; www.theroyaleast perth.com; daily 11am–late; bus: red CAT; map p.135 D2
The Royal occupies enviable waterfront real estate in East Perth. A range of beers on tap include WA's own Colonial Brewing, Under new ownership it is a popular restaurant, cocktail bar and pub.

Northbridge
The Brass Monkey
209 William Street, Cnr James Street; tel: 08-9227 9596; www.thebrassmonkey.com.au; daily 11am–late; train: Perth; map p.134 A3
The Brass Monkey is a Perth landmark and institution. Several different bar areas and plenty of Australian beers on offer, including many of Matilda Bay's beers on tap.
The Brisbane Hotel
292 Beaufort Street, Highgate; tel: 08-9227 2300; www.thebrisbanehotel.com.au; Mon–Tue 11.30am–late, Wed–Sat 11am–midnight, Sun until 10pm; bus: blue CAT; map p.134 B4

Below: in Venn, one of the trendiest spots in Perth.

below a gallery and behind a design-centric retail shop, DJs and musicians playing acoustic sets entertain patrons. In fair weather guests can hang out on the upstairs skydeck.
SEE ALSO SHOPPING, P.108
Wolfe Lane Bar
Wolfe Lane (access from Murray Street); tel: 9322 4671; www.wolfelane.com.au; Mon–Sat 4pm–late; bus: red CAT
Designed to be an intimate meeting place, Wolfe Lane is an atmospheric lounge-style bar tucked away off King Street, the CBD's premier shopping strip. It regularly hosts Perth's best DJs and it has a great cocktail list.

Leederville
The Garden
742 Newcastle Street; tel: 08-9202 8282; www.thegarden.net.au; Mon–Fri 11.30am–late, Sat–Sun 8am–late; train: Leederville
Located next to the iconic Leederville Hotel, The Garden is a relaxing outdoor courtyard, with bold coloured decor and wooden tables.

The restaurant serves food from breakfast on – the signature jug of Pimms is a crowd favourite.
Leederville Hotel
742 Newcastle Street; tel: 08-9286 0150; www.leederville hotel.com; daily 11am–midnight, Sun until 10pm; train: Leederville
The big nights here are Wednesdays and Sundays, when a young crowd packs out the beer garden in summer and the dance floor in winter. It caters to many moods: simply sit and have a quiet drink, enjoy a game of pool or get up and boogie.
Niche Bar
Off Oxford Street (city end); tel: 08-9227 1007; www.niche bar.com; Wed, Fri, Sat 7pm–late; train: Leederville
To find this hip bar walk through the car park at the end of Oxford Street, close to the station and freeway; 1970s style: white shag-pile and lots of couches.

East Perth
The Royal on the Waterfront
60 Royal Street; tel: 08-9221

Above: mojito at Llama Bar.

Possibly the most stylish hotel in Perth, the Brisbane is relaxed and funky. You can pop in for a drink, but the food is worth staying for, so grab a table in the shady garden. From a table you can get waiter service if you pop your credit card behind the bar.

Luxe Bar
446 Beaufort Street, Highgate; tel: 08-9228 9680; www.luxebar.com; Wed–Sun 8pm–late; bus: blue CAT; map p.134 C4

Luxe has mastered the art of cocktail couture and employs bartenders who have won awards for their craft. Plush, glamorous interior, gay- and straight-friendly.

The Queens
520 Beaufort Street, Highgate; tel: 08-9328 7267; www.the queens.com.au; Mon–Sat 10am–midnight, Sun 8.30am–10pm; bus: 67, 21

With a huge, leafy outdoor area, the Queens is a great spot for a cold beer on a sunny day. Inside, it's all about floorboards and rustic brick walls. Sample some of WA's best beer on tap here, from Matilda Bay Brewery.

Universal Bar
221 William Street; tel: 08-9227 6771; www.universalbar.com.au; Wed–Fri 3pm–late, Sat–Sun 5pm–late; train: Perth; map p.134 A3

Universal gets some great jazz and blues bands. An upstairs terrace bar is open at the rear. The small upstairs area features a section that opens up to the night sky in good weather.
SEE ALSO MUSIC AND DANCE, P.81

Subiaco

Llama Bar
1/464 Hay Street; tel: 08-9388 0222; Tue–Sat 5pm–late; train: Subiaco; map p.134 B2

It's an oldie, but the Llama is still one of the area's best bars. Owned by the same people behind the Subiaco Hotel, its recent face-lift makes it even slicker than before. Bar staff still mix some of the best cocktails in Subi.

The Subiaco Hotel
Cnr Hay and Rokeby streets; tel: 08-9381 3069; www.subiaco hotel.com.au; daily 7am–late; train: Subiaco; map p.132 B3

This pub has a couple of distinct drinking areas: a sports bar on one side and on the other, a designated chill area, with low-slung seats and couches. There is also a restaurant as part of the elegant building and the food is excellent. Popular on Fridays and after football games.
SEE ALSO RESTAURANTS, P.105

The Vic
226 Hay Street; tel: 08-6380 8222; daily 11am–midnight, Sun until 10pm; train: Subiaco; map p.132 C3

Excellent pub grub, and its outdoor garden is divine in good weather. Daily specials, and good lunch deals such as beer-battered fish and chips and a middy of Redback (a medium-sized glass of a local wheat beer) for just A$12.

> Several of Perth's big pubs are owned by the one group, ALH, so you will notice similarities between them, especially with the range of beers on tap. Some in the group include The Queens, The Vic and The Sail and Anchor.

Other dishes are always reliable. The bar packs out on a Friday night and whenever there's a game on at the nearby Subiaco Oval.

Fremantle

Little Creatures
40 Mews Road; tel: 08-9430 5155; Mon–Fri 10am–midnight, Sat–Sun 9am–midnight; train: Fremantle

You haven't truly experienced Freo's alternative vibe until you've visited Little Creatures. Located in an old boat shed, it's a restaurant, bar and working brewery, and always pumping. A great place to grab a pizza, share tapas and relax with an internationally awarded beer. Afterwards, head upstairs to Creatures Loft to enjoy the sweeping ocean views.

The Norfolk
47 South Terrace; tel: 08-9335 5405; Mon–Sat 11am–midnight, Sun 8.30am–10pm; train: Fremantle

The Norfolk's limestone-walled courtyard is a wonderful spot to while away a warm afternoon. The leafy outdoor area is often busy, but you'll find more room inside. The food is good-quality pub grub, ranging from light seafood to more substantial fare.

The Sail and Anchor
64 South Terrace; tel: 08-9335 8433; Mon–Thur 11am–midnight, Fri–Sat until 1am, Sun until 10pm; train: Fremantle

Perth's first microbrewery still produces great beers. A face-lift added a funky courtyard to complement the grand building. The upstairs area has a chilled bar feel, while downstairs it's more like a traditional pub.

Cottesloe, Claremont, Swanbourne and Scarborough

The Claremont

Cnr Bay View Terrace, Claremont; tel: 08-9286 0123; www.the claremont.com.au; Mon–Wed noon–midnight, Thur–Sat until 1am, Sun until 10pm; train: Claremont

A stalwart of the western suburbs' scene. Thursday is its biggest night, but you'll find people here at almost any time. The building is an old-style terrace, and punters sit outside on elevated boards just above street level.

Cottesloe Beach Hotel

104 Marine Parade, Cottesloe; tel: 08-9383 1100; www. cottesloebeachhotel.com.au; daily 11am–midnight, Sun until 10pm; train: Cottesloe, bus: 102

The Cott, as it's known, is packed out on fair-weather days. On Sunday afternoons the front terrace area packs out as people try to get a prime sunset-watching position, but there is a huge beer garden out the back, too. A young, lively crowd.

The Duchess

Claremont Quarter, Gugeri Street, Claremont; tel: 08-9384 4880; www.duchessbar.com.au; Tue–Sat noon–late; train: Claremont

The Duchess attracts an up-market crowd who come for the good tapas, wine and sophisticated ambience. High Tea is another highlight here.

Elba

29 Napoleon Street, Cottesloe; tel: 08-9284 2482; www.elbacottesloe.com.au; Mon–Thur 3pm–late, Fri–Sun noon–late; train: Cottesloe

This moody little bar in the heart of Cottesloe's hip Napoleon Street is a popular hang-out among Perth's beautiful people. For those not afraid of expanding waist-lines there are menus filled with tempting sharing and grazing plates. More substantial meals are also available.

Ocean Beach Hotel

Marine Parade, Cottesloe; tel: 08-9383 5402; www.obh. com.au; daily 11am–midnight, Sun until 10pm; train: Cottesloe, bus: 102

The OBH is a must-go for anyone wanting to experience a true piece of Australian pub culture. You'll fight to get space on a warm afternoon as customers jos-

tle to secure a prime location at the front of the bar, the place to be to watch the sun set over the ocean.

Swan Valley and the Perth Hills

Duckstein Brewery

9720 West Swan Road, Henley Brook; tel: 08-9296 0620; www.duckstein.com.au; Wed–Thur 11am–9pm, Fri–Sat until 11pm, Sun until 6.30pm; by car

This German brewery not only makes excellent beer, but has a huge list of German food to accompany it. The Brewer's Pan, a fry packed with pan-fried potatoes, kassler smoked pork cutlets and bratwurst sausages, is recommended.

The Kalamunda Hotel

43 Railway Road, Kalamunda; tel: 08-9257 1084; www.kalamundahotel.com.au; Sun 10am–10pm, Mon–Wed 11am–10pm, Thur–Fri 11am–late, Sat 10am–late; by car

The Kalamunda is an elegant building with good food to match. The menu features old favourites, including a beef-and-Guinness pie made from a secret family recipe. Beers on offer are your standard fare, with several UK beers on tap.

Below: the popular Little Creatures in Fremantle.

Restaurants

It has been said that Perth has more cafés and restaurants per capita than anywhere else in Australia. Whether that's true or not, there are a considerable number of great places to go and sate your hunger for something special. From adventurous Asian to classic Italian, Perth's multicultural bent has certainly paid off when it comes to dining. The city's proximity to the ocean makes seafood a natural highlight, as well as ensuring that there are eateries positioned in stunning locations overlooking the water. For further listings of establishments serving good food, see *Cafés, p.32–5,* and *Pubs and Bars, p.96–9.*

Swan River and Kings Park

EUROPEAN
Zafferano
173 Mounts Bay Road, Crawley; tel: 08-9321 2588; www.zafferano.com.au; daily 11am–late, breakfast from 8am; $$$$; bus: 102, 103, 24; map p.137 D4
Located in the historic Swan Brewery complex, this high-end restaurant has some of the prettiest views of the city at night. The menu offers classic Italian seafood dishes,

including melt-in-your-mouth crayfish and seafood risotto. The atmosphere and service are up-market, so it's perfect for a special dinner. Ask for a table with a view.

MODERN AUSTRALIAN
Balthazar
6 The Esplanade; tel: 08-9421 1206; Mon–Fri noon–3pm, Mon–Sat 6–10pm; $$$$; train: Perth; map p.134 A2
You won't find Balthazar just by walking past, but it's worth the effort to look for it. Conveniently located in the CBD on the corner of Howard Street and only a short stroll across the grass from the Swan Bell Tower, this dark, sophisticated restaurant serves some of the best food in town. Known for a massive and interesting wine list, and waiters who are very knowledgeable and happy to advise. Perfect for the indecisive are the tasting plates, which change daily (they even have a dessert tasting plate). Balthazar is a must for foodies, and it is best to book.

Left: a glass of wine and a light bite at Fraser's Restaurant.

Fraser's Restaurant
Fraser Avenue; tel: 08-9481 7100; ww.frasersrestaurant. com.au; daily noon–late; $$$$; bus: 102, 78, 24, 37; map p.133 D1
Executive Chef Chris Taylor is a proud advocate of top-quality Western Australian produce, and you'll find plenty of it at the renovated Fraser's. Expect a varied menu with a dedicated char-grill section and a mains list full of organic, locally farmed chicken, lamb and beef. The restaurant has the best views in town – situated high up in Kings Park it overlooks the city and Swan River.

Halo
2 Barrack Square at Barrack Street Jetty; tel: 08-9325 4575; www.halorestaurant.com.au; Mon–Sat lunch noon–3pm, dinner 6pm–late; $$$; bus: blue CAT; map p.134 A1
Located at the Barrack Street Jetty, with great views of the river (ask for a table with a river view). This is a fine-dining restaurant without any pretensions, with most mains coming in around A$40. Where possible, free-range

Left: fine dining at Halo.

MODERN AUSTRALIAN
Bar One
Lower level, QV1 building, 250 St George's Terrace; tel: 08-9481 8400; www.bar1.com.au; Mon–Fri 7am–late; $$$; train: Perth; map p.133 E2

This funky bar-cum-café attracts people at all times of day. You can pop in for a coffee and have a bite to eat, a more serious pasta lunch, or relax over drinks with a group of friends at the end of the day. It is popular on Friday nights with young professionals, so if you don't want shoulder-to-shoulder action choose another night to visit. The food is Italian-influenced – try the angel hair pasta with crab.

Greenhouse
100 St George's Terrace; tel: 08-9481 8333; www.greenhouse perth.com; Mon–Tue 7am–late, Wed–Sat 7am–midnight; $$$; train: Perth; map p. 132 A2

Vertical gardens spill down the walls of this eco-friendly favourite. A rooftop veggie patch provides produce for the kitchen and the tapas-style menu offers goodies such as spiced pumpkin with eggplant (aubergine), chickpeas and fried quinoa.

Approximate cost of main meal with a glass of wine:	
$$$$	A$50 plus
$$$	A$40–50
$$	A$20–35
$	less than A$20

and organic products are used. You will often find top quality beef cuts and seafood on the menu.

Matilda Bay Restaurant
3 Hackett Drive, Crawley; tel: 08-9423 5000; www.matbay. com.au; daily 11am–late; $$$; bus: 102, 103, 24; map p.136 A1

Situated on the banks of the Swan River at Matilda Bay, this restaurant is popular for its beautiful views and peaceful location, making it a good option for a special occasion at reasonable cost. Market fresh seafood and fresh local produce are features of the contemporary menu and the extensive wine list offers an impressive selection of wines.

City Centre

JAPANESE
Matsuri
Lower level, QV1 building, 250 St George's Terrace; tel: 08-9322 7737; www.matsuri.com.au; Mon–Sat noon–2.30pm, 6–10pm; $$; bus: red CAT; map p.133 E2

A great spot for a fast and tasty Japanese meal that won't break the bank. Entrées such as the beef tataki are good to share, and the set menus (choice of mains such as ginger fish or chicken teriyaki, plus miso soup, rice and salad) offer good value. The quality is excellent for the price – it is flavoursome and generous.

Taka's Kitchen
397 Murray Street (in Shafto Lane); tel: 08-9324 1234; www.takaskitchen.iinet.net.au; Mon–Sat 11am–9pm; $; bus: blue CAT; map p.134 A2

You'll fight to get a table at this popular, cheap Japanese café at lunch time. With an emphasis on speed and value, it serves a range of dishes (including agedashi tofu, chicken katsu, teriyaki fish and sashimi). All meals are available in small or large sizes. There is free tea and a range of help-yourself sauces. The quality is reasonable, especially at such low prices.

> In better restaurants in Perth, BYO ('bring your own' alcohol) is not permitted. Occasionally BYO wine is accepted, but there is often a stiff corkage fee to deter people from doing this. However, there are some gems where they don't mind if you bring your own wine and the corkage is often very reasonable, so definitely ask when you call to book, and ask what the corkage charges are (even though most bottles of wine in Australia now use a stelvin (screw-cap) seal, so technically there is no actual cork to deal with).

101

Above: a room with a view.

Lamont's Bishop's House
Cnr Spring Street and Mounts Bay Road; tel: 08-9226 1884; www.lamonts.com.au; Mon–Fri for lunch and dinner; $$$$; train: Perth; map p.133 E2

Surrounded by high rises and the hustle and bustle of the CBD this is a stunning restaurant set in a historic 100-year-old former private residence. Owned by local foodie, Kate Lamont, the restaurant sees guests dine in a selection of meticulously restored dining rooms, or on a splendid verandah overlooking a heritage-listed garden. The food is spectacular.

Leederville

EUROPEAN
Duende
662 Newcastle Street; tel: 08-9228 0123; www.duende.com.au; daily 7pm–late; $$$; train: Leederville

This surprising nook of a restaurant ticks lots of boxes. Atmosphere? Definitely. Top-notch food? Certainly. Amazing wine list? Of course. Duende is a little slice of Europe, serving fabulous tapas, cheese and other titbits in an elegant yet funky setting. Ask for some help with the wine list and perhaps even let the waiter choose for you. It is the sort of place to enjoy a long leisurely evening with lots of tapas and divine wine, and good conversation with friends.

FISH
Kailis Bros Fish Café
101 Oxford Street; tel: 08-9443 6300; www.kailisbros leederville.com.au; daily 7am–late; $$; train: Leederville

On one side of the store is a market counter selling some of the best fresh seafood in WA, and on the other side is a seafood restaurant. The Kailis family is one of the biggest local players in seafood, and you will be guaranteed excellent quality, whether it's a fried snapper fillet or fresh tuna sashimi. They also serve great breakfasts. There is another branch in Fremantle but the dining is far more casual.
SEE ALSO FOOD AND DRINK, P.60

SOUTHEAST ASIAN
Kitsch Bar
229 Oxford Street, Leederville; tel: 08-9242 1229; www.kitsch bar.com.au; Tue 5–10.30pm, Wed–Sat 5–11.30pm; $$$; train: Leederville

Approximate cost of main meal with a glass of wine:	
$$$$	A$50 plus
$$$	A$40–$50
$$	A$20–35
$	less than A$20

With an Asian night market feel, this spicy, opium den-like venue serves hawker-inspired Asian tapas. Everything here is spot on, but the pad Thai and spiced corn fritters with green chilli coriander syrup are house favourites. The restaurant is closed on Monday when it conducts its popular cooking classes.

Ria
106 Oxford Street; tel: 08-9328 2998; www.riarestaurant.com.au; Tue–Sat 6–10pm, Sun–Mon 5.30–10pm; $$; train: Leederville

If you have any interest in Malaysian food, put Ria on your list of places to visit. From salty chunks of fish served on banana leaves to Mother's moist, caramelised duck, you'll find it difficult to choose just a few dishes. The atmosphere is modern. Be sure to book.

East Perth

MODERN AUSTRALIAN
Friends Restaurant
Hyatt Regency, 20 Terrace Road; tel: 08-9221 0885; www.friends restaurant.com.au; Mon–Fri noon–3pm, 6pm–late, Sat–Sun 6pm–late; $$$$; bus: 39, 106, 177; map p.135 C1

This is undeniably one of Perth's poshest restaurants, featuring a massive wine list of aged, rare and simply stunning wines. Many of them are stored in a purpose-built cellar off-site simply because they have too many to keep here. The food is similarly extravagant – Wagyu beef fillet with blue cheese croquette, tomato fondue, cauliflower gratin and red wine jus; and pork belly with sage and onion compote, caramelised apple, creamed potato and apple balsamic dressing.

Restaurant Amuse
64 Bronte Street, East Perth; tel: 08-9325 4900; www.restaurant

amuse.com.au; Tue–Sat
6.30pm–late; $$$$; train:
Claisebrook; map p.135 D2

Lauded as having the best
dégustation menu in Perth,
Restaurant Amuse is quickly
becoming a local institution.
There is no à la cart menu,
and the dégustation will set
you back a pretty penny, but
food critics all agree that this
is a fine dining experience not
to be missed. Allergies and
dietary requirements are dis-
cussed at time of booking.

Rockpool

Crown Perth, Burswood; tel: 08-
6252 1900; www.rockpool.com;
daily noon–3pm, 6pm–late;
$$$$; bus: 24, 296

If you appreciate great steak,
you simply can't go past
Rockpool, which serves the
best in town. Owned by
celebrity chef, Neil Perry, it
sources only the very best
cuts and offers treats such as
the 80-day dry-aged rib eye
on the bone.

SOUTHEAST ASIAN
Yú

Burswood Entertainment Complex, Burswood Hotel, Burswood;
tel: 08-9362 7551;
www.burswood.com.au/Restaur
ants/Premium/YU; daily
noon–3pm, 6pm–late; $$$$;
bus: 24, 296

Offering some of the best
Cantonese cuisine in Perth,
Yu's tends to take classic Chi-
nese dishes and give them a

contemporary twist. Signature
dishes include melt-in-your-
mouth Szechuan sliced fillet
steak, Portuguese stuffed
crabs and Peking duck. Service is slick and the wine list is
extensive.

JAPANESE
Nobu

Crown Perth, Burswood;
tel: 08-9362 7551;
www.burswood.com.au/Restaur
ants/Premium/Nobu; Tue–Sat
noon–3pm, daily 6pm–late;
$$$$; bus: 24, 296

Considerable fanfare wel-
comed the opening of Nobu in
late 2011 and the hype was
met with some of the most
elegant, fresh and revolutionary Japanese fusion cuisine
the city had ever seen. Nobu's
dining room is stunning, the
cocktails are incredible and
the service is second to none.

Northbridge

INDIAN
Gogo's Madras
Curry House

556 Beaufort Street, Highgate;
tel: 08-9328 1828; Mon–Sat
6pm–late; $$; bus: 60

The Indian cricket team dine
here when in town. Gogo
cooks seriously good food,
with the menu extending
beyond the obvious fare.

ITALIAN
Il Padrino

94 Aberdeen Street, Northbridge;

tel: 08-9227 9065;
www.ilpadrinocaffe.com; Tue–Fri
11am–late, Sat 5pm–late; $$,
bus: blue CAT; map p.134 A3

The walls of this pizzeria tell its
story: everyone who is anyone
has acknowledged just how
good Nunzio's pizzas are. The
Pizza Association of Sicily has
even declared him the best
pizza-maker in the world.

Below: exquisite food, lovingly
prepared and elegantly served,
at Friends Restaurant.

Maurizio

235 Fitzgerald Street, Northbridge; tel: 08-9228 1646; www.mauriziorestaurant.com; Tue–Fri noon–3pm, 6pm–late, Sat 6pm–late; $$$; bus: 363, 60; map p.134 A4

Fine dining inspired by regional Italian food. Menus are created seasonally, but dishes such as the roast baby goat and braised rabbit are staples on the menu.

MODERN AUSTRALIAN
Jackson's

483 Beaufort Street, Highgate; tel: 08-9328 1177; www.jacksons restaurant.com.au; Mon–Sat 7–10.30pm; $$$$; bus: 60

One of Perth's top places to dine. Chef-owner Neal Jackson likes to pair unusual combinations, such as apple risotto with grilled chorizo and seared scallops, and bluecheese balls dipped in dark chocolate. This is another essential visit for those looking for a top-notch experience.

Must Winebar

510 Beaufort Street, Highgate; tel: 08-9328 8255; www.must. com.au; daily noon–midnight; $$$$; bus: 60

Join Highgate's cool kids in the funky front bar with a glass of wine, or settle down

for a serious bistro-style meal in the restaurant. Must has a 500-bottle wine list, and upstairs there is an ask-to-enter champagne lounge where you can enjoy select bubbles by the glass (or bottle). Labels include Salon, Ruinart, Delamotte, and heavy hitters such as Krug, Dom Perignon and Cristal.

SOUTHEAST ASIAN
Little Saigon

489 Beaufort Street, Highgate; tel: 08-9227 5586; Tue–Sun 5.30–10pm; $$; bus: 60

This little restaurant has a groovy red-and-white fit-out and serves authentic Vietnamese food. Try the prawns on sugar cane starter and the goat-and-eggplant curry. Good value and you can BYO.

Nahm Thai

223 Bulwer Street, Highgate; tel: 08-9328 7500; Wed–Sat 6pm–late; $$$; bus: 60; map p.134 B4

This must be the best mod-Thai restaurant in Perth. The dishes are innovative and delicious – from the rich duck-and-lychee curry to the tangy galloping horses (mandarin topped with minced pork and chilli).

The Red Teapot

413 William Street; tel: 08-9228

Approximate cost of main meal with a glass of wine:	
$$$$	A$50 plus
$$$	A$40–$50
$$	A$20–35
$	less than A$20

1981; www.redteapot restaurant.com.au; Mon–Sat 11.30am–3pm, 5.30–10pm; $$; bus: blue CAT; map p.134 B4

Small and funky, this local favourite serves great Hong Kong-style Chinese. There are a few signature dishes, including honey king prawns and salt-and-chilli squid. Booking advisable.

Viet Hoa

349 William Street; tel: 08-9328 2127; www.viethoa.com.au; daily 10am–10pm; $; bus: blue CAT; map p.134 B3

The biggest Vietnamese restaurant in Northbridge. It's a far cry from fine dining, but the food is decent and cheap.

Subiaco

JAPANESE
Cheers

375 Hay Street; tel: 08-9388 2044; Mon–Fri 11.30am–2.30pm, 6pm–late, Sat 6pm–late; $; train: Subiaco; map p.132 B3

This authentic Japanese restaurant is hidden behind a group of shops on Hay Street. If you're with a group, make sure you ask for one of the traditional tables where you take off your shoes and let your feet dangle into the well under the table. Order a range of things to share.

Nippon Food

479 Hay Street; tel: 08-9388 2738; Mon–Sat 11am–4pm; $; train: Subiaco; map p.132 B3

This postage stamp-sized eatery produces tasty teriyaki chicken for busy office crowds

Left: Perth offers some great waterside dining opportunities.

all week. It also has a range of inexpensive sushi. It has just three tables out front, so you might be better off getting takeaway and heading for one of the nearby parks.

INDIAN
Chutney Mary's
67 Rokeby Road; tel: 08-9381 2099; www.chutneymarys. com.au; Mon–Sat noon–2.30pm, 5.30–10.45pm, Sun 5.30–10.45pm; $$; train: Subiaco; map p.132 B3

The fragrant smells wafting out of this Indian restaurant on the corner of Hay and Rokeby will entice you off the street. The thali plates are a popular lunch option, and at under A$15 are good value: choose between meat, fish or vegetarian curries; you'll also get rice, naan, dahl, soup and dessert.

ITALIAN
Funtastico
12 Rokeby Road; tel: 08-9381 2688; www.funtastico.com.au; daily 8am–late; $$; train: Subiaco; map p.132 B3

If you can get up-market casual, this is it. Favoured by folk-about-town for its good pastas and sensational pizzas, it has great alfresco seating.

Galileo
199 Onslow Road, Shenton Park; tel: 08-9382 3343; Tue–Fri noon–3pm Tue–Sat 6pm–late; $$$; train: Shenton Park

Serves elegant Italian cuisine, and definitely worth a visit. Those who like more unusual combinations will be kept happy, along with the more average palates. Not an easy balance to maintain, but they do it well. Staff are lovely and servings are generous.

MODERN AUSTRALIAN
Bistro Felix
118–20 Rokeby Road; tel: 08-9388 3077; www.bistro; daily noon–late; $$$–$$$$; train: Subiaco; map p.132 B3

Bistro Felix is the place to come for refined Mod Oz cuisine. Chef Damien Young places emphasis on using produce in season, so the menu changes regularly, but expect lovingly executed dishes such as raviolo of prawn, creamed corn with celery and sauce noire, and crisp confit of pork belly and vegetables 'en barigoule' with green tomato chutney. The wine list is huge and considered and includes a handful of producers exclusive to the restaurant.

Purl Bar
71–5 Rokeby Road; tel: 08-9381 7755; www.purlbar.com.au; Mon–Fri from noon for lunch, Mon–Sat from 5.30pm, Fri–Sat 9.30pm–1am; $$$; train: Subiaco; map p 132 B3

In the heart of Subi, this brand new, laid-back bar and restaurant serves Middle Eastern inspired food and chargrilled meats and has a sophisticated, glamorous vibe. It also has a late night menu (very unusual for Perth) and an unusual cocktail list.
SEE ALSO NIGHTLIFE, P.85

The Subiaco Hotel
Cnr Hay Street and Rokeby Road; tel: 08-9381 3069; www.subiacohotel.com.au; daily 7am–late; $$; train: Subiaco;

> New to Western Australia is a website that can assist with your eating requirements. Eating WA is an online resource that provides punters with the opportunity to read and post their own reviews of the restaurants they visit. You'll find star ratings as well as commentary, but as with all reviews, make sure you take them with a pinch of salt. You can search for restaurants by name, cuisine and location. See: **www.eatingwa.com.au**.

Above: elegance at Jackson's.

map p.132 B3

Known just as 'The Subi', this pub-cum-restaurant is always busy, and deservedly so. The inventive, inspired food ranges from Moroccan seafood tagine with spinach and feta brik pastry and twice-cooked pork belly, with prawn and scallop caramel sauce and steamed rice cake. Booking advisable.
SEE ALSO PUBS AND BARS, P.98

The Witch's Cauldron
89 Rokeby Road; tel: 08-9381 2508; www.witchs.com.au; daily 7.30am–late; $$$; train: Subiaco; map p.132 B3

This restaurant has been on the Perth scene for longer than most people can remember. It is famous for its garlic prawns, steaks and seafoods. Not the most innovative cuisine, but reliable and loved by many.

Fremantle
EUROPEAN
George Street Bistro
73 George Street, East Fremantle; tel: 08-9339 6352; www.george-street.com.au; Mon–Fri 7.30am–3pm, Tue–Sat 6pm–late, Sun 8am–5pm; $$$; bus: 106

The walls are brightly coloured and adorned with artwork, the food robust German-Euro fare. There are some big flavours

105

here, especially in the signature duck with braised red cabbage and sauerkraut. Very popular with locals.

FISH
Cicerello's Fish and Chips
44 Mews Road, Fisherman's Wharf; tel: 08-9335 1911; www.cicerellos.com.au; daily 10am–late; $; train: Fremantle

A family favourite that has been serving fish and chips for longer than anyone can remember. Refurbished and extended, it has several magnificent fish tanks (the fish are decorative, not dinner) that you can watch while you queue. Dine alfresco and soak in the Freo Wharf atmosphere.

Kailis Fish Market Café
46 Mews Road, Fishing Boat Harbour; www.kailis.com; tel: 08-9335 7755; daily 8am–late; $; train: Fremantle

Kailis has been providing Perth and Fremantle with seafood for over 75 years *(see also p.102)*. The fresh seafood market resides at one end of the large store and the café functions at the other, with ample seating outside on the jetty. There's basic fish and chips, plus a variety of salads, grills and desserts.

The Mussel Bar
42 Mews Road, Fishing Boat Harbour; tel: 08-9433 1800; www.musselbar.com.au; Mon 6pm–late, Tue–Sun noon–late; $$; train: Fremantle

The atmosphere here is bright and cheerful during the day and more intimate at night. The creative menu makes the most of fresh local seafood, but includes meat alternatives as well. Eat overlooking Fremantle Harbour.

INDIAN
Maya
77 Market Street; tel: 08-9335 2796; www.mayarestaurant.

com.au; Tue–Sun 6pm–late; Fri noon–late; $$$; train: Fremantle

This multi-award-winning restaurant combines a modern, elegant interior and classic Indian food. The flavours range from intense to subtle – if you prefer heat, you'll find it, and if you like fragrant you'll be satisfied, too. Try the house speciality goat dish or the chilli whiting fillet and hot Tawa scallops.

ASIAN FUSION
Barque
125 George Street, East Fremantle; tel: 08-9339 5524; www.barquerestaurant.com.au; Wed–Sat 8am–11pm; Sun 9am–4pm; $$$; bus 106

Serving Asian fusion tapas, this newcomer has gained a reputation for perfectly executed food, and a relaxed vibe. Everything is tasty, but it's hard to better the crispy duck and shitake spring rolls and Asian-style pancakes.

MODERN AUSTRALIAN
Harvest
1 Harvest Road, North Fremantle; tel: 08-9336 1831; www.harvestrestaurant.net.au; Tue–Thur 6pm–late, Fri–Sun 8am–late; $$$; train: North Fremantle

Located in a quirky old cottage, with mismatched furniture, Harvest takes diners on an interesting culinary journey, exploring all sorts of styles and flavours along the way. The food, however, is anything but chaotic. The breakfasts are delicious, and it's worth trying the rustic-style dishes at lunch and dinner. Produce is home-grown on a vacant lot next door.

Sandrino Café
95 Market Street; tel: 08-9335 4487; www.sandrino.com.au;

daily 11am–late; $$ train: Fremantle

A popular Fremantle eatery influenced by the flavours of the Adriatic. It prides itself on its authentic wood-fired pizza and fresh local seafood. The service is fast and friendly, with a bustling atmosphere that oozes Fremantle. And there's a lounge bar next door.

SOUTHEAST ASIAN
Sala Thai
22 Norfolk Street; tel: 08-9335 7749; www.salathai.com.au; daily 6pm–late; $$; train: Fremantle

Sala Thai offers authentic Thai flavours in a relaxed setting. The staff are friendly and the food has a lovely fresh zing so typical of Thai. Good-quality ingredients and attentive service.

Cottesloe, Claremont, Swanbourne and Scarborough

MODERN AUSTRALIAN
Beluga
Claremont Quarter, Gugeri Street, Claremont; tel: 08-9383 1638; www.belugaclaremont.com.au; Tue–Sat noon–late; $$$; train: Claremont

Located in the trendy new

Right: the Indiana Tea House at Cottesloe Beach *(see page 29)*.

Claremont Quarter shopping precinct, Beluga offers a rich dining room with cosy nooks where tables of two can enjoy an intimate evening out. With a focus on fresh produce, the menu also has a list of exclusive caviars.

Il Lido

88 Marine Parade, Cottesloe; tel: 08-9286 1111; daily 7.30am–late; $$$; bus: 102, 103

This funky café-cum-restaurant with its communal tables is directly opposite Cottesloe Beach, and they're happy for you to stroll in, sandy feet and all. The menu is exceptional, which is rare for a place with such a good view. Expect crab, lime and chilli linguine and Wagyu beef papardelle. Excellent wine list.

Lamont's Wine Store

12 Station Street, Cottesloe; 08-9385 0666; www.lamonts.com.au; daily noon–late; $$$; train: Cottesloe

Owned by Western Australian fresh food ambassador, Kate Lamont, this little 'wine bar meets bistro' is a great place to share a quick bite with friends, a more leisurely meal and a glass of top-quality wine. The wine list showcases top international and national producers, and all can be purchased for takeaway from the wine store.

Mosman's

15 Johnson Parade, Mosman Park; tel: 08-6365 5140; www.mosmans.com.au; Thur–Sun noon–2.30pm, Mon–Sun 6–9pm; $$$; train: Mosman Park then walk 1.5km (1 mile); bus 102 or 99 to Walter Street then walk 1.5km (1 mile).

You don't get much prettier than this riverside restaurant in the affluent suburb of Mosman Park. Literally built over the water, this is a great place to soak up Perth's glorious Swan River with a relaxed meal and top-quality glass of wine.

Van's

1 Napoleon Street, Cottesloe; tel: 08-9384 0696; Sun–Thur 7am–10pm, Fri–Sat 7am–10.30pm; $$$; train: Cottesloe

This café epitomises the best that restaurants in Perth have to offer: a relaxed atmosphere, top-quality produce served in original ways, good wines, and great coffee to finish off. The duck spring rolls as an entrée are fantastic, the open sandwich with organic chicken and roast capsicum is a perfect light lunch, and the dinner menu is mouth-watering.

Approximate cost of main meal with a glass of wine:
$$$$ A$50 plus
$$$ A$40–$50
$$ A$20–35
$ less than A$20

Swan Valley and the Perth Hills

FRENCH
The Loose Box

6825 Great Eastern Highway, Mundaring; tel: 08-9295 1787; www.loosebox.com.au; Wed–Sat 6pm–late, Sun noon–3pm; $$$$; by car

Award-winning French cuisine in idyllic surroundings. Celebrity chef Alain Fabrègues uses only top-quality ingredients, including home-grown organic herbs and vegetables to create his incredible French dégustation menu. Make a night of it by staying in one of the beautiful on-site chalets.

MODERN AUSTRALIAN
Dear Friends

100 Benara Road, Caversham; tel: 08-9279 2815; www.dearfriends.com.au; Wed–Sun noon–late; $$$$; by car

Dear Friends is responsible for some of the best, most surprising and innovative food in Perth, run by a dynamic young couple who have made the drive out to 'the valley' well worth the effort. The eight-course dégustation is the speciality. A three-course option is also available.

Darlington Estate

39 Nelson Road, Darlington; tel: 08-9299 6268; Wed–Thur and Sun noon–3pm, Fri–Sat noon–3pm, 6pm–late; $$$; by car

The food at this winery restaurant is sublime. The style is European, with well-balanced flavours. The signature dish is a lamb shank wrapped in pastry. The wines are good and the views are beautiful.

SEE ALSO WINE COUNTRY, P.128

107

Shopping

The shopping scene in Perth is very healthy, with new shops opening regularly, including big-name brands such as Gucci, Hugo Boss, Tiffany & Co. and Bally. Until 2007 Perth's only luxury brand was Louis Vuitton, which has occupied space on the exclusive King Street strip since 1997. The arrival of these heavy-hitters indicates that Perth's economy is flush and people are spending big. But it's not only international brands – small retailers with quirky flair are opening throughout suburbs like Northbridge where rents are considerably lower than in the city or in the major shopping centres.

Antiques

Guildford's shops have the most variety – not by any means all fine, or even antique, but definitely interesting. Where else would you buy an ex-RAAF padded bag designed for parachuting crockery and cutlery? Opposite Guildford train station a dozen shops stock bric-a-brac and antiques. More are over the railway in Swan Street. Happy hunting can be done on Queen Victoria Avenue, North Fremantle, too. Here a

Several shopping malls and arcades lie between St George's Terrace and Wellington Street, each with their own individual character. Trinity Arcade has three levels containing essential services, as well as treats such as rare books, antiques, fine menswear, jewellers and more. Piccadilly, Plaza and Carillon City are the other principal arcades. Many of the stores located within these arcades are not life-changing, but you will find some interesting buys nonetheless.

line of antique dealers sells all manner of furniture, lights, jewellery and other treasures.

Scurrs Antiques

769 Beaufort Street, Mount Lawley; tel: 08-9272 5181; Mon–Sat 10am–5pm, Sun 11am–5pm; bus: 67, 21

This shop sells antique, Victorian, Edwardian and 1920s furniture brought over from the UK.

Turnstyle Collectables

155 Stirling Highway, Nedlands; tel: 08-9386 7088; www.turnstylecollectables.com.au; Tue–Sat 10am–5pm, Sun noon–5pm; bus: 102 and 103 to Robinson Street

Set within an old cottage, Turnstyle has one of the most eclectic and exciting collections of antiques and collectables in Perth. Also in Northbridge, 173 William Street; tel: 08-9228 1026; Mon–Fri 10am–6pm, Sat 10am–5pm; train: Perth.

Arts

Perth embraces the arts and throughout the city, especially in the CBD, you will find good-quality galleries and arty retailers.

Art Gallery of WA shop

Perth Cultural Centre, 47 James Street Mall; tel: 08-9492 6766; www.artgallery.wa.gov.au; Wed–Mon 10am–5pm; train: Perth; map p.134 B3

Stocks books on art, architecture and gardening, catalogues of exhibitions, notepaper, prints and designer gifts.

SEE ALSO MUSEUMS AND GALLERIES, P.76

Aspects of Kings Park

Fraser Avenue, Kings Park; tel: 08-9480 3900; daily 9am–5pm; bus: 37 and 39 (free from the CBD); map p.133 D1

This gallery and retail space overlooking the city in Kings Park houses only the highest quality contemporary Australian and Western Australian craft and design.

Creative Native

Shop 58, Forrest Chase, Perth; tel: 08-9221 5800; www.creativenative.com.au; Mon–Thur 9am–5.30pm, Fri until 6.30pm; Sat until 5pm, Sun 11am–5pm; train: Perth; map p.134 A2

A great range of authentic Aboriginal art, objects and didgeridoos.

Left: shopping for antiques and bric-a-brac.

Sales seem to happen frequently – especially in the large department stores. Expect an end-of-financial-year stocktake sale, a pre-Christmas sale, an even better post-Christmas sale, plus end of season sales. Good savings can be found, especially on homewares such as bed linen, crockery, knives and cookware.

Myer has fought hard not to be seen as David Jones's poor cousin and finally, they're winning the battle. These days, both stores stock a good range of Australian designers in dedicated sections. Myer has great sales and has them often – mid-year, end of year, end of season and so on.

Markets

For market updates see www.marketsonline.com.au.
E Shed Markets
Victoria Quay, Fremantle; www.eshedmarkets.com.au; Fri–Sun 9am–5pm, food court until 8pm; train: Fremantle
A 100-year-old converted wharfside cargo shed with fresh produce, beauticians, Australian bush goods, sheepskin, metal-craft, numerology, tarot and psychic readings.

Fremantle Arts Centre Shop

1 Finnerty Street, Fremantle; tel: 08-9432 9569; daily 10am–5pm; www.fac.org.au; train: Fremantle
One-of-a-kind locally sourced gifts including jewellery, textiles, ceramics, glassware, wooden items and books.

Venn

16 Queen Street, Perth; tel: 08-9321 8366; www.venn.net; Mon–Thur 9am–5pm, Fri until 7pm, Sat 10am–5pm; train: Perth; map p.134 A2
This hub of creativity houses an art gallery, artists' studios a café/bar and design shop. Encased in glass, the spectacular store is jam-packed with exclusive international homewares and unusual gift ideas.

Department Stores

David Jones

622 Hay Street Mall; tel: 08-9210 4000; www.davidjones.com.au; Mon–Wed 9.30am–7pm, Thur–Fri until 9pm, Sat 9am–5pm, Sun 11am–5pm; train: Perth city; map p.134 A2

David Jones's flagship store faces onto the Hay Street Mall, its large picture windows displaying of-the-moment designers. There is an incredible basement food hall, overflowing with great lunch ideas and gourmet take-home meals. David Jones considers itself the more up-market of the mall's two department stores, generally stocking more expensive options.

Myer

200 Murray Street; tel: 08-9265 5600; www.myer.com.au; Mon–Thur 9am–6pm, Fri until 9pm, Sat 9am–5pm, Sun 11am–5pm; map p.134 A2

Right: Hay Street Mall.

Mon–Thur 9am–5.30pm, Fri until 9pm, Sat 9am–5pm, Sun 11am–5pm; train: Perth; map p.133 E2

One of several stockists of hardcore outdoor wear on this part of Hay Street.

R.M. Williams

Carillon Arcade, Hay Street; tel: 08-9321 7786; www.rmwilliams.com.au; Mon–Thur 9am–5.30pm, Fri until 9pm, Sat 9am–5pm, Sun 11am–5pm; train: Perth; map p.134 A2

R.M. was a 'real' Aussie who became the 'bushman's out-fitter' by providing solid and reliable kit, from boots, sad-dles and whips to hats and swags (bed-rolls) for rough Australian outback condi-tions. This is now an inter-national retailer with outlets across the Western world.

Quirky Finds

Black Plastic

226 Carr Place, Leederville; tel: 08-9328 1236; Mon–Fri 10.30am–5pm, Thur until 8pm, Sat 10am–5pm, Sun 10.30am–4pm; train: Leederville

An odd little gift shop with a huge range of quirky cards. Expect to find Jesus toys next to handbags and old movie posters.

Test Tube

6/595 Beaufort Street, Mount Lawley; tel: 08-9228 1118; www.testtubeobjects.com.au; Mon–Sat 10am–5.30pm, Thur until 7pm; bus: 67, 21

This design-focused store sells a great range of gifts, or simply things with which to spoil yourself. The owners travel the world sourcing interesting design pieces – from jewellery to homewares, ties to beauty products. The fit-out won a commercial design award.

Fremantle Markets

South Terrace, Fremantle; www.fremantlemarkets.com.au; Fri 9am–8pm, Sat–Sun 9am–6pm, fresh food market daily from 8am; train: Fremantle

Recently renovated it has handmade and natural organic produce, health food, pottery, finely crafted jewellery, clothing, fresh fruit and vegetables and a good range of food – the crêpes are ever popular.

SEE ALSO FOOD AND DRINK, P.60

Station Street Markets

41 Station Street, Subiaco; www.subiacomarkets.com; Fri–Sun, Mon (public holidays) 9am–5.30pm; train: Subiaco; map p.132 B4

A wide range for sale, includ-ing small furnishings, clothes old and new, books, records,

as well as a large selection of fresh fruit and vegetables.

SEE ALSO FOOD AND DRINK, P.61

Outback Style

Australian Geographic

Carillon City; tel: 08-9318 1307; www.australian geo-graphic.com.au; Mon–Thur 9am–5.30pm, Fri until 9pm, Sat 9am–5pm, Sun 11am–5pm; train: Perth; map p.134 A2

The eclectic stock here is cer-tain to throw up an unusual, Australian-accented gift, such as soundtrack CDs of frogs croaking, or rock crystals that replace deodorant.

Mountain Designs

862 Hay Street; tel: 08-9322 4744; www.mountaindesigns.com; Mon–Thur 9am–6pm, Fri until 9pm, Sat 9pm–5pm, Sun 11am–5pm; train: Perth; map p.134 A2

Supplies professional-level outdoor clothing you could take up Everest.

Paddy Pallin

884 Hay Street; tel: 08-9321 2666; www.paddypallin.com.au;

> Bigger branches of **R.M. Williams**, like that in Carillon City, stock a wide range of Aussie icons, such as the Driza-Bone waxed stockman's coat and the fur-felt Akubra hat.

A referendum in 2007 saw WA vote against extended trading hours, which would have seen larger shops and suburban retailers allowed to trade more extensively on Sundays and late at night. Some wanted Perth to have more flexibility for the workforce who struggle to get to the shops in normal hours; others wanted to protect those who would end up working to accommodate the extended trading times.

Above: an unmistakable souvenir from your Australian trip.

Shopping Centres

Claremont Quarter
Bayview Terrace, Claremont tel: 08-9286 5888; www.claremont quarter.com.au; Mon–Sat 9am–5.30pm, Thur until 9pm; train: Claremont; bus: 98 and 99
Perth's newest shopping precinct has found favour with well-heeled Perthites. It's home to a plethora of top-end designers including Carla Zampatti, Sass & Bide, Alannah Hill, Karen Millen and Marcs, as well as lots of local favourites.

enex100
Hay Street Mall, Perth; www.enex100.com.au; Mon–Thur 9am–5.30pm, Fri until 9pm, Sat 9am–5pm, Sun 11am–5pm; train: Perth; map p.134 A2
The enex100 complex links Hay Street Mall to St George's Terrace and offers three storeys of food and retail outlets including Calvin Klein, Lisa Ho, and GUESS.

Garden City
125 Riseley Street, Applecross; tel: 08-9364 7911; www.garden city.com.au; Mon–Fri 9am–5.30pm, Thur until 9pm, Sat until 5pm; bus: 940, 881
An older shopping centre that had a dramatic face-lift and is home to many quality retailers. As with many such centres, it's usually only national chains that can afford the rent. Here you'll find Myer and David Jones (see p.109), as well as a large range of fashion, homewares, sporting goods, jewellery and other retailers. There's a cinema complex next door.

Karrinyup
Karrinyup Road, Karrinyup; tel: 08-9445 1122; www.karrinyup centre.com.au; Mon–Fri 9am–5.30pm, Thur until 9pm, Sat until 5pm; train: Clarkson, bus: 425, 426, 423
Another older centre that has experienced an upgrade. There are some interesting retailers selling clothes, shoes and homewares, and department stores Myer and David Jones (see p.109).

Westfield Carousel
1382 Albany Highway, Canning-ton; tel: 08-9458 6344; www. westfield.com.au/carousel; Mon–Fri 9am–5.30pm, Thur until 9pm, Sat until 5pm; bus: 220
A massive American-style shopping centre featuring a cinema complex, a large range of food options and many shops. Definitely not top-end, and gets incredibly busy, but it's very affordable. However, it is quite a drive from the city.

Sports

Perth, like all of Australia, is sports-mad. The most popular spectator sports are Australian Rules Football (AFL) during winter and cricket in summer. If you want to make friends with local people, especially men, you need to know what's going on, or at least be a keen student (and barrack for their team). Often the most diehard fans look like they've never thrown a ball or run a metre in their life. As for participant sports, the range is large, and during the better weather months there is a large range of competitions just about every weekend, including ocean swims, triathlons, running and lots of team sports.

Aussie Rules Football

Australian Rules Football is Perth's most popular spectator sport. AFL is a winter sport, running from March through to the Grand Final at the beginning of October. Western Australia has two national teams, the **West Coast Eagles** and the **Fremantle Dockers**, vying for local support. The Eagles are the older of the two teams, and have several premiership titles under their belt, the most recent being in 2006. The Dockers are yet to win a premiership; however, they are a strong team. Each plays home games at **Patersons Stadium** (otherwise known as Subiaco Oval) and local club games (WAFL–WA Football League) are played all around Perth. Memberships are sold to the teams, and this accounts for most of the 40,000-odd seats at Subiaco Oval, but each week a section is reserved for public ticket sales (at one end of the oval behind the goals). This allows fans of visiting teams, and people who have not been able to secure, or who cannot afford, a membership to attend a game. Games that are sold out are broadcast live on free-to-air television.

Patersons Stadium

Between Subiaco Road and Roberts Road, Subiaco; tickets: 1300-135 915; www.westcoast eagles.com.au or www.fremantlefc.com.au; train: Subiaco; map p.132 B4–C4
Tickets are around A\$35 for an adult and can be purchased through www.ticket master.com.au/afl or at the ground.

Left: a Kangaroo Aussie Rules ball.

Diving

Dive sites are located all around the WA coast, with many close to Perth. Local dives include Rottnest and Carnac islands, and extend as far as Dunsborough and Rockingham. You can also dive in the big tank at the Aquarium of Western Australia. Around Perth the diving season is October to May. Further north, at Coral Bay, Broome and Exmouth, the season is much shorter.

Perth Diving Academy
283 Wanneroo Road, Balcatta; tel: 08-9344 1562; www.perth diving.com.au; bus: 388 (from Wellington Street Bus Station) to Wanneroo Road

Runs diving courses and international package tours as well as stocking all the equipment, for sale or hire, you will require.

Horse Racing

Perth has two racetracks, both just a short ride from the city centre. **Ascot**, with its outdoor bars and restaurants, is used for summer meetings. **Belmont Park** is on the river, with enclosed facilities to keep the punters warm and dry in the winter. Entry is generally free midweek, unless there is a special meeting, and remains cheap (around A$10) at weekends. Ascot's **Perth Cup**, on 1 January every year, is the racing and fashion highlight of the season. **Melbourne Cup** (the first Tuesday in November) is known as 'the race that stops a nation', and indeed it is. The biggest party on the day is at Ascot, and by the end of the day you will find many bedraggled women in cocktail dresses and fascinators in pubs around town.

Patersons Stadium – otherwise known as Subiaco Oval – celebrated 100 years in 2008. The stadium had a significant overhaul in the early 1990s, but is due for redevelopment. A new football stadium is to be built on the Burswood Peninsula at a cost of around $700 million.

Basketball

Perth Wildcats is WA's team in the National Basketball League. Their home base is at **Challenge Stadium**, but they often tour around Western Australia.

Challenge Stadium
Mount Claremont, Stephenson Avenue; tel: 08-9441 8222; www.wildcats.com.au; bus: 27, 28

Cricket

The **WACA ground** (Western Australian Cricket Association) is HQ of state cricket and the venue for all important matches – state, championships,

Left: serious business at the WACA and a friendly game in the park.

international one-day, the new 20–20 format and Test matches. But high-standard matches featuring state players in their local club teams can be seen across Perth on summer weekends. The **Lilac Hill** ground in Guildford is one of the finest, worth a visit for its lovely setting by the river. Another is in the grounds of the University of WA, Crawley.

Lilac Hill
West Swan Road, Caversham; train: Guildford, then free shuttle bus

WACA Ground
Nelson Crescent, East Perth; tel: 08-9265 7222; www.waca.com.au; bus: red CAT; map p.135 D1

Cycling

Bicycles can be hired from **About Bike Hire**. There are numerous bike paths around the river, which make for a relaxing, picturesque activity. A comprehensive government site is www.dpi.wa.gov.au/cycling.

About Bike Hire
Point Fraser Reserve, Riverside Drive, Perth; tel: 08-9221 2665; www.aboutbikehire.com.au; bus: blue CAT; map p.139 C4

113

Ascot

70 Grandstand Road, Ascot; tel: 08-9277 0777; www.perth racing.com.au; bus: 299 or check transperth.wa.gov.au for special arrangements on big race days

Belmont Park

Victoria Park Drive (off the Graham Farmer Freeway), Tel: 08-9470 8222; www.perth racing.com.au; train: Belmont Park; map p.135 E4

Horse Riding

Various riding schools are located around Perth; to hire a horse for a good long ride you will have to go out of town.

The Stables Yanchep
Yanchep Beach Road; tel: 08-9561 1606; train: Joondalup
Hire a horse for a minimum of two hours and roam over trails and deserted beaches. Courtesy bus is available from Joondalup rail station if you reserve when booking. Fee is moderate.

Horse Riding Perth
62 Park Street, Henley Brook, tel: 08-9296 1222, www.horse ridingperth.com.au; Tue, Thur, Sat 9am–6pm; by car
Affordable riding lessons catering to riders of all levels, including children.

Running and Jogging

Running is popular in Perth, and the 10km (6-mile) circuit around the bridges is well used. The biggest public run is the annual **City to Surf** which is held at the end of August. Runners start in the city on St George's Terrace, making their way through Subiaco, Floreat and ending at City Beach.

The run is 12km (7.5 miles), but there is also a 4km (2.5-mile) walk option, an 11km (7-mile) wheelchair option, a half-marathon 21.1km (13-mile) and a new marathon 42km (26-mile) option.

Soccer

Soccer is slowly gaining ground in Western Australia. The state team is **Perth Glory**, based at NIB Stadium.

NIB Stadium
310 Pier Street, East Perth; tel: 08-6218 4203; www.perth glory.com.au; buses run especially during seasonal games, check http://transperth.wa. gov.au; map p.134 B3
Tickets can be purchased through the team's website. Local teams play on grounds across the city.

Surfing

Reliable conditions mean you can catch a wave all year in WA, though would-be surfers would be wise to check first with the experts at Surfing WA (tel: 08-9448 0004; www.surfing australia.com). Courses (for ages 8–70) are held at Trigg Beach, which with Scarborough has Perth's best surf. South of Perth, Yallingup and Lancelin are noted for bigger waves, and Margaret River is

Left: taking the plunge in the Rottnest Channel. The February swim is a major event *(see below)*.

Royal Kings Park Tennis Club
Kings Park Road, West Perth; tel: 08-9321 3035; web n/a; bus: red CAT; map p.133 D2
The club is used for major competitions, such as the Davis Cup.

Triathlon
The triathlon (swim, ride, run) is well supported in Western Australia, with the season running from October to early May (www.triwa.org.au). Distances vary, but the big ones to aim for are the **Busselton Half Ironman**, which is held in early May, and the **Ironman Western Australia**, also in Busselton (www.ironman westernaustralia.com) in December. The half distances are 1.9km (1.2-mile) swim, 90km (56-mile) ride and 21.1km (13-mile) run. The full Ironman distances are, of course, are double this.

on the international circuit. Heading north, Lancelin is also good.

Indian Ocean temperature doesn't vary much in WA, but the wind chill does, and many surfers use wetsuits here. Surfing Australia will advise on shops that rent out suits and boards.

Adrift
190 Scarborough Beach Road, Mount Hawthorn; tel: 08-9444 5399; www.adrift surfing.com; Mon–Fri 9am–4pm, Sat 9am–2pm; bus: 400 (to Scarborough Beach where lessons are held)
Runs very reasonably priced surf tours and camps – one, two or three days – including transport to Lancelin, accommodation and meals, as well as four hours of lessons every day.

Swimming
Australian waters can be hazardous. In Perth, go to a beach that's guarded by surf life-savers, and swim

between the red-and-yellow flags that mark their surveillance area.

Clean, well-maintained public swimming pools are located in most parts of Perth. The main one, used for championship events with indoor and outdoor pools, is at Challenge Stadium.

Challenge Stadium
Mount Claremont, Stephenson Avenue; tel: 08-9441 8222; www.venueswest.wa.gov.au; bus: 27, 28

Tennis
Many tennis clubs in Perth welcome visitor players. Suburban courts can also be hired for a fee; the details are usually posted on the fencing, and often a local deli collects money and distributes keys.
The **Hopman Cup** (www.hopmancup.com) is Perth's big international tennis tournament, played by mixed doubles in December and January at the Burswood Dome.

Burswood Dome
Crown Perth; tel: 08-9362 7777; www. burswood. com.au; bus: 296

Left: cycling and jogging along the Swan River.

Each February around 2,000 swimmers leave the safety of Cottesloe Beach and swim to Rottnest Island. The swim is approximately 20km (12.5 miles), and you can opt to do it solo, in a duo or a team of four. The fastest are usually the solo swimmers, with the best time recorded being around the four-hour mark. A team of four average swimmers could expect to take seven to eight hours, depending on weather. All swimmers have a boat, support crew and a paddler, and sharks are asked not to attend. The first wave of swimmers leaves the beach around 6.45am; if you are in Perth in mid-February, check the date and go and wave the brave swimmers off.

Theatre

Diverse productions are staged all year throughout the city, with a strong avant-garde scene supported by small companies and semi-professional groups. Perth has also begun to attract a good range of international productions, especially during February's Perth International Arts Festival *(see Festivals, p.54)*, where you can soak up everything from Korean versions of Shakespeare to Scottish plays about war. Perth has a well-patronised local scene, too, with several plays on at any given time. For more information on the performing arts, *see Music and Dance, p.80–3.*

Companies

Barking Gecko
180 Hamersley Road, Subiaco; tel: 08-9380 3080; www.barkinggecko.com.au; train: Subiaco; map p.132 A2
This production company specialises in children's theatre. It also travels to schools to give workshops, and hosts workshops for ages 5–17, teachers and professionals.

The Blue Room Theatre
53 James Street, Northbridge;

tel: 08-9227 7005; www.pacs.org.au; train: Perth; map p.134 A3
The Blue Room is the trading name for the Performing Arts Centre Society, which is a membership-based, not-for-profit organisation. Formed in 1989, it offers WA performing artists a support network, and gives Perth audiences a wide range of eclectic shows.

Deckchair Theatre
179 High Street, Fremantle; tel: 08-430 4771; www.deckchairtheatre.com.au; train: Fremantle
Deckchair is one of WA's most awarded companies, and focuses on West Australian stories wherever possible.

Perth Theatre Company
Cnr William and Roe streets, Perth; tel: 08-6212 9339; www.perth theatre.com.au; train: Perth; map p.134 A3
Perth Theatre Company has been producing professional theatre in Western Australia since 1983. The vision is about developing new West Australian theatre and supporting local artists. The impressive new, architect-designed centre features a range of unusual performance spaces including the Black Box, the Studio Underground, a purpose-built outdoor events area called The Courtyard, the Heath Ledger Theatre, two rehearsal rooms and two flexible-use private suits. PTC tours annually throughout regional Western Australia, visiting small, isolated areas as well as large

Left and below left: the Perth Theatre Company.

Regal Theatre
Cnr Hay Street and Rokeby Road; tel: 08-9381 5522; www.regaltheatre.com.au; train: Subiaco; map p.132 B3
The Regal is a heritage-listed Art Deco building and attracts a quirky range of shows, often musicals, comedy and other entertaining productions, generally not overly highbrow.

Spare Parts Puppet Theatre
1 Short Street, Fremantle; tel: 08-9335 5044; www.sppt.asn.au; train: Fremantle
As the name suggests, Spare Parts is dedicated to puppetry. Its shows are written for children, yet work on levels where adults get something out of them, too. Spare Parts is considered one of Australia's top puppet theatres – in 2008 it hosted the World Puppetry Congress, which saw a solid calendar of public events that attracted adults and children alike. They also had a crack at setting a Guinness World Record – a million puppets in one place at the same time in Perth's Concert Hall.

Yirra Yaakin Aboriginal Theatre
3/9 Brook Street, East Perth; tel: 08-9221 9688; www.yirrayaakin.asn.au; train: Claisebrook; bus: red CAT; map p.135 C2
Yirra Yaakin is considered one of Australia's premier Aboriginal theatre groups. It is highly awarded and tells compelling tales of historical and contemporary Aborigines. If you can manage to get to one of their shows, it is well worth it.
SEE ALSO ABORIGINAL CULTURE, P.27

For the biggest range of tickets across theatre, dance and music go to www.bocsticketing.com.au or call 08-9484 1133. Most theatres use this centralised service.

cities and towns. It also tours nationally and internationally.

Theatres

His Majesty's Theatre
825 Hay Street, Perth; tel: 08-9265 0900; www.hismajestystheatre.com.au; train: Perth; map p.134 A2
His Majesty's Theatre is a grand building located on the corner of Hay and King streets in the city. Some see it as an over-the-top, wedding cake-style building, but you can't deny it has a sense of grandeur. Marble staircases lead to the higher levels of the building, while inside the theatre red carpet is the theme, with small ornate balconettes overlooking the stage. Underneath the theatre there is a small space called Downstairs at the Maj where a series of contemporary performances are staged.
SEE ALSO MUSIC AND DANCE, P.80

Quarry Amphitheatre
Reabold Hill, Oceanic Drive, City Beach; tel: 08-9385 7144; www.quarryamphitheatre.com.au; bus: 85
On the slopes of Reabold Hill, this amphitheatre is hemmed in by towering limestone walls and has tiered grassy levels. You can see the city skyline from the top of the arena, and in summer a series of intimate concerts is held here, as well as theatre productions.

The **West Australian Academy of Performing Arts** is regarded as one of Australia's top training grounds for actors, directors, producers and anyone involved in the performing arts. Entry is highly competitive, and often it will take several attempts before admission is offered. WAAPA (pronounced 'whopper') is part of Edith Cowan University, and boasts alumni such as Australian actors Hugh Jackman and Marcus Graham.

Transport

As the most isolated capital city in the world, it's hard to get to Perth by any environmentally friendly means. Generally visitors need to fly in, even if coming from another state in Australia, as the drive is long. The nearest capital city is Adelaide in South Australia, and that is 3,194km (1,996 miles) away. Once you are in Perth, you can access the main tourist sites easily by train. The trains are electric, fast, clean and new. Hiring a car is a good way to get around, too, and gives you the flexibility to maximise your time. Although Perth's traffic is heavy during peak times (7.30–9am, then 4–6pm) the city is easy to navigate.

Getting There by Air

INTERNATIONAL

Airlines are virtually the only way into Perth from abroad. Occasional cruise ships dock at Fremantle, but unless you have lots of time to spare, it has to be a plane. There are 17 international airlines that fly into Perth. Most direct flights from Europe are routed via Singapore, while another popular route is via Dubai with Emirates, which divides the trip into two more equal legs.

Air Mauritius
Tel: 08-9486 9133;
www.airmauritius.com

Air Asia
Tel: 1300-760 330;
www.airasia.com

Getting to Perth will almost certainly require flying, and if not, some form of extensive rail or car travel will be the second option. Regardless of how you get to Perth, it is worthwhile investigating how to offset your carbon footprint. www.carbon neutral.com.au is a good place to start, as is http://carbon offsetguide.com.au.

Air New Zealand
Tel: 13 24 76; www.airnew zealand.com.au

British Airways
Tel: 1300-767 177; www.ba.com

Cathay Pacific
Tel: 13 17 47; www.cathay pacific.com.au

China Southern
Tel: 1300-889 628;
www.csair.com/en

Emirates
Tel: 1300-303 777;
www.emirates.com/au

Garuda Indonesia
Tel: 1300-365 331 or 08-9214 5101; www.garuda-indonesia.com

Jetstar
Tel: 13 15 38; www.jetstar.com

Malaysia Airlines
Tel: 13 12 23;
www.malaysiaairlines.com

Qantas
Tel: 13 13 13;
www.qantas.com.au

Qatar Airways
Tel: 1300-240 600;
www.qatarairways.com/au

Singapore Airlines
Tel: 13 10 11; www.singapore air.com.au

South African Airways
Tel: 08-9216 2200; www.fly saa.com

Thai Airways
Tel: 1300-651 960; www.thai airways.com.au

Tiger Airways
Tel: 03-9999 2888;
www.tigerairways.com

Virgin Australia
Tel: 13 67 89;
www.virginaustralia.com

DOMESTIC

If you're already in Australia there are direct flights from all other major cities with Qantas, Virgin Australia and Jetstar (see above for all). Virgin Australia and Jetstar usually have cheaper flights, but do not include in-flight catering or entertainment. Skywest offer a top-class service within the state.

Skywest
Tel: 1300-660 088;
www.skywest.com.au

AIRPORT

Perth Airport (www.perth airport.com) is currently undergoing a multimillion-dollar upgrade of its terminals, services and access routes. The Domestic and International terminals are about 5km (3 miles) apart. If you are

Left: boarding a busy Transperth train.

FROM THE DOMESTIC TERMINAL

In addition to the shuttle services, Transperth bus 37 operates daily between the Domestic Terminals and Kings Park, via Belmont Forum Shopping Centre, Victoria Park Transfer Station and the Esplanade Bus Port. The journey takes approximately 55 minutes. The domestic terminals are located about 10km (6 miles) from the city centre, and a taxi will cost around A$35.

Getting There by Train

Railway buffs consider the Indian Pacific railroad to be one of the world's great rides. Well, it's certainly long. **Great Southern Railway** (tel: 13 21 47; www.great southernrail.com.au) operates the twice-weekly service into Perth from Sydney, via Adelaide and Kalgoorlie.

The full journey of 4,352km (2,704 miles), much of it through the Nullarbor Desert, takes 64 hours and can be done in varying degrees of comfort, from sit-up-and-ache seats to more luxurious private sleeper compartments.

Flights to and around the north of Western Australia are regular and reliable, because of the stream of fly-in/fly-out workers at the mines. Qantas also services internal flights in WA, as do a number of other reputable companies *(see left for details)*.

connecting with a flight, a free shuttle bus operates between the two every 50 minutes, or as demanded. The trip takes just eight minutes with shuttle stops located right at the front of each terminal. Otherwise taxis link the two locations.

FROM THE INTERNATIONAL TERMINAL

If you're travelling between the International Airport and the city centre, taxi is by far the post popular option. The International Terminal is 13km (8 miles) from the city centre and taxi fares are about A$45. From Fremantle the fare is slightly more expensive.

Perth Airport Connect shuttle busses (www.perth airportconnect.com.au) are another reliable and cheaper alternative. Picking travellers up from their hotel door, or residential addresses in the Fremantle area, the shuttles are comfortable, air-conditioned buses that are guaranteed to get you there on time. From the city the service costs $15 to the domestic and $18 to the international terminal. From Fremantle you will pay a flat fee of $33 regardless of the terminal you need to go to. Bookings are essential.

Right: Transperth Rail's Esplanade Station.

Getting There by Road

Coach services across the Nullarbor Desert from the eastern states have been abandoned, but one quirky option remains. You could arrive from the north. **Greyhound Pioneer** (tel: 13 20 30; www.greyhound.com.au) runs long-haul buses from Adelaide to all major cities east and north, so travellers could take the scenic route, north to Darwin, thence to Kununurra, Broome, Exmouth and down to Perth.

DRIVING

Driving to Perth from the eastern states is considered a rite of passage for many Australians. Perth to Adelaide is 2,642km (1,642 miles); to Melbourne 3,375km (2,097 miles); to Sydney 3,902km (2,425 miles). Although there's a lot of featureless desert on the Nullarbor, you can make occasional diversions to the southern coast. Before considering the driving option take full safety advice from motoring organisations; and compare hire/fuel costs with internal flight deals.

Getting Around

BY BICYCLE

Cycling paths have been developed all around Perth, alongside the freeway, coast and even into the hills and

Transperth helps passengers with disabilities to access trains. Call 1800-800 022 an hour in advance and a customer service officer will meet you at the station. Prams and wheelchairs are easily accommodated on trains, ferries, CAT buses and the new green-and-silver Mercedes fleet of buses. But some older buses don't have extendable ramps; Infoline will give information on which routes do.

cross-country. One path leads around the Swan in central Perth and all the way down to Fremantle. The **Perth Bicycle Network** (www.dpi.wa.gov.au/cycling) is a useful source of information. Maps are available from bike shops, or the **Bicycle Transportation Alliance** (2 Delhi Street, West Perth; tel: 08-9420 7210). **About Bike Hire** (see Sports, p.113) rents bikes, double bikes, and quad-cycles – with trailers or baby seats.

BY BOAT

Cruising down the river is an excellent way to get to Fremantle, taking in views of Kings Park, Melville Water and the coves and beaches on both sides of the Swan. Both **Oceanic Cruises** (tel: 08-9335 2666; www.oceaniccruises.com.au) and **Captain Cook Cruises**

(tel: 08-9325 3341; www.captaincookcruises.com.au) offer one-way or return trips, including tea/coffee and commentary. They take around an hour each way; Captain Cook throws in a free wine-tasting on the return leg.

BY BUS

Transperth (InfoLine: 13 62 13) runs city buses, trains and the ferry. Transperth has an excellent website that can plan your journey for you, www.transperth. wa.gov.au.

Central city bus travel is free in the inner zone, which includes most parts visitors will want to see. Traffic jams are few, and buses are plentiful, so this is a quick way around town. The free service applies to all regular buses while they're in the central zone, as well as CATs. The free CATs (Central Area Transit) are distinctive buses – red, blue or yellow, depending on the route – linking the main tourist sights and running from early morning until early evening. Computer read-outs and audio messages at their dedicated bus stops tell you when the next CAT is due (generally within five minutes).

Most other bus routes head out of Perth in a radial pattern, which is fine for tourists heading for the beaches, Fremantle, etc. There are fewer services circling the city from suburb to suburb.

Tickets

Bus ticket prices depend on how many zones your journey covers. Pay the driver as you board the bus. Train and ferry tickets are bought at self-service machines.

DayRider tickets are good value for unlimited, day-long

Left: light traffic and dedicated lanes makes cycling easy.

Right: open-top bus tours are a quick way to gain your bearings.

travel on all Transperth services after 9am weekdays and all day at weekends and on public holidays. SmartRider electronic ticketing is a quick, cash-free system for use on any Transperth bus, train or ferry service.

BY CAR

Australians drive on the left, as in the UK. Hiring a car offers flexibility and convenience. If your driving licence is written in English you can use it in Australia for three months. An international driving permit will always be acceptable.

Remember there will be variations in road rules in Australia, and they can vary between states. WA's rules can be checked on the government website www.onlinewa.com.

A few pointers: seat belts must be worn by driver and passengers; drivers must indicate lane-changing and never change lane in immediate vicinity of traffic lights or junctions. Perth's speed limit is 60kmh (about 36mph) unless otherwise signed. 'Local' streets will have 50kmh (30mph) signs; school zones are 40kmh (25mph). The top speed in the country is 110kmh (about 70mph) on open country roads where signed. On the freeway it's only 100kmh (about 60mph).

Major car hire firms in Perth are **Avis** (toll-free: 1800-812 808; www.avis.com.au), **Budget** (tel: 13 27 27; www.budget.com.au) and **Hertz** (toll-free: 1800-550 067; www.hertz.com.au). Others include **Thrifty** (tel: 1300-361 351; www.thrifty.com.au/wa) and **Europcar** (tel: 1300-131 390; www.europcar.com.au). All are at various easily accessible locations. Camper van and motorhome specialists include **Britz** (toll-free: 1800-331 454; www.britz.com.au), **CampaboutOz** (tel: 08-9331 6500; www.campaboutoz.com.au) and **Wicked Campers** (toll-free: 1800-2468 69; www.wicked campers.com), whose vans come multicoloured, with graffiti, for the young at heart.

BY FERRY

Perth's only regular ferry is also operated by Transperth, between **Barrack Street Jetty** on the north side of the Swan and **Mends Street Jetty** in South Perth. The ferry is a pleasant approach to the restaurants, bars, pubs and shops on the South Perth Esplanade and Perth Zoo.

BY TAXI

Hail taxis on the street, find them on a rank, or call **Black and White** (tel: 08-9333 3333) or **Swan** (tel: 13 13 30). Rates are reasonable, a small flagfall charge followed by a rate per kilometre. Expect a long wait on Friday and Saturday nights. Download the Swan Taxi app for faster service.

BY TRAIN

Wellington Street is the central station, with an underground terminal for the Mandurah line. Modern air-conditioned trains run south through Perth to Fremantle, north to Joondalup, and down the coast to Mandurah. It's a comfortable and efficient way to travel, especially during the day.

ON FOOT

Although Perth has long been known as a city for cars, it is small, the weather is usually fine and walking is safer here than in many cities. Equipped with a sunhat, sunglasses, sunblock and a bottle of water, you will be fit for anything. Free walking tours are available with City Perth volunteers. Meet at the booth opposite the Commonwealth Bank buildings in Murray Street Mall, Mon–Sat 11am.

Right: underground rail line.

Walks and Views

With districts often divided by rail lines and freeways, making it hard to wander seamlessly between neighbourhoods on foot, it has been joked that Perth is a city for cars; for a city with so many outdoor glories, it has not been known for easily accessible walks. However, this is changing. Footpaths and bike paths have become more prevalent, and with the upcoming sinking of the Northbridge Link, accessibility will undoubtedly increase. In the meantime, there are some peaceful and interesting walks to be found, and great vantage points to get that photo-perfect view over Perth.

City Views

Start: Barrack Street/Riverside Drive; map p.134 A1
End: Riverside Drive/Causeway; map p.139 D4

At the corner of Barrack Street and Riverside Drive, near the Swan Bell Tower, are the Supreme Court Gardens. These beautiful gardens play host to outdoor concerts in fair weather, but make for a worthwhile stop year-round. The gardens contain the **Supreme Court** and the City of Perth's oldest building, the original **Court House**. Now known as the Francis Burt Law Education Centre, it was built in 1836 and was the only building available for public meetings at the time of being built. It's also been a church, boys' school, law court and now houses a small museum (Mon–Wed, Fri 10am–2.30pm).

From the Supreme Court Gardens walk across to the **Swan Bell Tower** (see p.6). Heading east along the river's edge, you will pass **Langley Park** on your left. Langley Park was created by land reclamation between 1921 and

Above: view over Perth.

1935 and was originally used as an air-strip. Today, it's a popular spot to watch the **Australia Day** fireworks on 26 January (see Festivals and Events, p.54), and also plays host to games of polo, touring circuses and other events.

At the end of Langley Park on the riverside is **Point Fraser**. Recent works at Point Fraser have seen a new wetland created and connected by boardwalks. All along this path you get a wonderful view across the Swan River to South Perth, with the full height of the

Kings Park escarpment behind you.

Kings Park Riverside and Tree-Top Walk

Start: Riverside Path, Kings Park; map p.137 D4
End: University of Western Australia; map p.136 A2

This walk offers lovely views over Perth's main green space in the city, Kings Park. Traverse the Tree-Top Walk for views over the canopy of trees and shrubs. The building glimpsed through the foliage on the left is the **Old Brewery**. Restored after years of controversy – Abo-

Left: footpaths and bike paths make walking a pleasure.

If it's a guided walking experience you're after, **Two Feet and Heartbeat** (www.twofeet.com.au) offers a range of tours in the CBD. For a taste of the best places to shop, join the Murray to King Street Tour, every Saturday morning at 10am. Guests meet their own personal style consultant then make their way through the malls. The tour finishes with a relaxing lunch on King Street *(See also Fashion, p.52–3)*

riginal people claim this site is the sacred home of the Wagyl, a mysterious snake-like creature that created rivers by meandering over the land – it is now an up-market complex of shops, restaurants and apartments. Depending on the time of day, there could be countless yachts on this stretch of river. You may also see the **Duyfken**, a replica of the ship in which the Dutch mariner Willem Jansz became the first European to record a landing in Australia, in 1606, 164 years before Cook's famous landing in Botany Bay.

From here, you can also visit the **University of Western Australia**, taking a 20-minute stroll through the bush. Native bush plants edge the path all the way, olive and sage-green rather than the lusher northern hemisphere emeralds. Some of the most distinctive are the banksias, with their cone-shaped flowers, palm-like zamias and grass trees, with their mop of spiky grass, which are known as 'the

coconut of the southwest' because of the many uses Aboriginal people make of them. Forest fires stimulate the growth of grass trees, blackening the fire-resistant trunks and lending them the common, if un-PC, name of 'blackboy'.

At the end of the park, turn left into Park Avenue, one of the most exclusive areas in the city. The administration buildings and residential colleges of the university (UWA) line the avenue all the way to Winthrop Avenue. Of these, **St George's College**, with its

crenellated towers and flag-pole, is the most picturesque. SEE ALSO CAFÉS, P.32

Northbridge Heritage Walk

Start: James Street; map p.134 A3
End: Newcastle Street/William Street; map p.134 B3

Though it hums at night, Northbridge by day is sedate. When colonists arrived, the area was swampy lakeland, but in the 1840s it was drained, and market gardens flourished in the rich soil. Building spread north from the river and central Perth, and in 1861 the railway was taken through. After this,

Below: at the University of Western Australia.

W

people began talking about 'north of the line' and eventually, Northbridge.

West along James Street, opposite Rosie O'Grady's is leafy **Russell Square**, a traditional meeting place for Aboriginal people and now, with its elegant town houses and new builds, a meeting place for just about everyone. Central to the rejuvenated square is the Pagoda artwork and bandstand, where concerts are regularly held. The cast-iron artworks represent WA's development and Northbridge's diversity: the granite galleon symbolises European influence; the pagoda the Asian community's impact on the area; the bronze snake and bearded dragon represent the natural environment; and a child's school bag, hope for the future. Fun and entertainment are represented by a bush hat, towel and sunglasses *(see picture, below)*.

Walk further along James Street, checking the **Breadbox** and **Fusebox** galleries on the way to Fitzgerald Street. Part of **Artrage**, an alternative arts organisation based near the **Western Australian Museum**, these galleries often have avant-garde shows on.

A right turn on Fitzgerald leads to St Brigid's Church and the **Piazza Nanni**, named in honour of Father Nanni, St Brigid's parish priest for many years. Built on land reclaimed when the Graham Farmer Tunnel cut through Northbridge, the granite piazza contrasts with the traditional red-brick and sandstone church buildings.

Look down onto the freeway emerging from the tunnel. This was Perth's biggest road-building enterprise in years. It cut a swath through Northbridge, taking out many old buildings, but also opening up new areas such as Piazza Nanni, and **Plateia Hellas** on Lake Street *(see p.14)*.

New streets bearing the names of notable local citizens reflect the international diversity of the area: Kakulas Court, Hoy Poy Street, Via Torre, Grigoroff Road and Zempilas Road among them.

Opposite Piazza Nanni is the start of the **Aberdeen Street Heritage Precinct**, with colourful houses and shops in a range of architectural styles. Many eminent

early Perthites chose to live here, away from the bustle of the city. The shops and houses at the west end of Aberdeen were less grand, generally built as matching pairs in federation Queen Anne, bungalow or free Classical style. The most striking of these (No. 182) is the bright blue-painted antique shop of Vincenzo Rizzo, built for Braddock's Dispensary in the 1890s (the name can still be seen in the upper masonry).

A 'modern' Art Deco iron fence and gate, incorporating aircraft, cars and plant motifs, is a later addition to the well-balanced double-fronted No. 176. Victorian Italianate style is in evidence at Nos 162 and 166, both dating from the gold boom and prosperous early 1890s.

Palmerston Street (north, off Aberdeen) is filling with new apartments. At the far end, the historic Union Maltings has been restored, turning rambling factories into new homes. Some units retain huge steel girders running through the walls, and solid jarrah floors. There's a small museum of artefacts and photographs of 1900s maltings operations, and sculptures made from industrial bits and pieces spread around the complex.

On the east corner where Newcastle Street crosses Palmerston is a small heritage precinct of cottages by the Perth architect Sir J.J. Talbot Hobbs. The small houses on Newcastle Street recall the start of Hobbs's career as an architect, when the population boom of the early 1890s inspired building in some unlikely locations. Hobbs built his cottages in modest Federation Bungalow style as investments to rent

Below: one of the cast-iron works in the Pagoda.

Left: walking past The Brass Monkey pub *(see Pubs and Bars, p.97)* in Northbridge.

vated gardens, a wonderful place to stop and enjoy views of the Indian Ocean, distant Rottnest Island, and the busy shipping lane into Fremantle.

Napier Street, alongside the north wall, will take you down to the ocean and Marine Parade. Turn to walk along the front, past pubs, cafés, restaurants and shops towards **Indiana Tea House**, a good spot to refuel with coffee and cake. This is the most popular part of **Cottesloe Beach**, with a paddling pool, volleyball courts and good swimming.

When returning to the station, you could live dangerously and walk through the attractive golf course along Jarrad Street. Look out for flying balls; you can keep all you catch.

SEE ALSO BEACHES, P.28

out. The contrast with his great works – such as the **WA War Memorial** in Kings Park, the Weld Club and the **Savoy Hotel**, couldn't be greater.

Follow Newcastle back to the entertainment area of Northbridge, via William Street. Upper parts of many Perth commercial establishments are original work from the gold-rush era. A newer one in striking Art Deco with an impressive vertical clock can be seen above a pizza shop, where Newcastle meets William.

SEE ALSO MUSEUMS AND GALLERIES, P.77–8

Cottesloe Town and Beach Walk

Start/End: Cottesloe Station
Cottesloe is a popular and well-established small town with only 7,000 residents and many superior dwellings in a short coastal strip. The towering Norfolk pines you'll see on most streets have become something of an icon, a long-

lasting symbol of the town. Many houses are in the turn-of-the-19th century federation style, tastefully mixed in with modern developments.

At Cottesloe Station, cross the railway line on Jarrad Street and walk west towards the ocean. Jarrad Street will take you up to the Sea View Golf Course to the ocean, but stop short of the links and turn right on Broome Street to see the most splendid council offices in the state.

The Cottesloe Civic Centre is a 1911 Spanish-style mansion within Gothic balustraded garden walls, and set in spacious terraced gardens. Tycoon Claude de Bernales built the villa, wrapping it around the 1898 home of a one-time WA attorney-general. The grounds and walls date back to the original. As the buildings are in daily use by council staff, they aren't open to the public, but nobody will object if you wish to linger in the ele-

Mundaring and Kalamunda are centres in an area rich in natural attractions. As well as local walks – in Fred Jacoby Forest Park, or on the abandoned Jorgensen Park golf course, there is the 1,000km (620-mile) Bibbulmun Track, which begins in Kalamunda. Meandering through the wild and picturesque countryside of the southwest, it is one of the world's great long-distance trails. It could take eight weeks to reach Albany on the south coast, but sections can be covered in shorter time-frames (there are cabins for overnight stops). For options, including single-day walks without a pack, contact the Bibbulmun Track Foundation (tel: 08-9481 0551; www.bibbulmuntrack.org.au).

Wine Country

Australia's largest state has nine wine-growing regions and more than 350 wineries, almost entirely concentrated in its southwest corner. Though they account for just 3 percent of Australia's wine production, they produce 20–30 percent of the country's premium vintages. Wine is big business in WA, and most wineries will have a cellar door where you can try and buy. There has been a lot of effort put into making cellar doors attractive; some are nothing short of splendid. Tastings are mostly free, although on more expensive wines you may have to pay a small fee, usually around A\$2–3, to be waived if you purchase.

Great Southern

Adjacent to Margaret River, the Great Southern region is noted for Cabernet wines of deep colour and intense flavour, as well as for Rieslings and Chardonnays. It also produces a small amount of high-quality Shiraz, with some promising Pinot also emerging. **Taste Great Southern**, a massive region-wide festival in February and March, shows off the area's burgeoning food and wine industries (www.greatsouthern

tastewa.com)

Alkoomi
1141 Wingebellup Road, Frankland River; tel: 08-9855 2229; www.alkoomi wines.com.au; daily 10am–4pm; by car
Alkoomi's wines are held in great esteem, with the cool climate of the region lending itself to sumptuous reds and a beautiful Riesling.

Ferngrove
276 Ferngrove Road, Frankland; tel: 08-9855 2378; www.ferngrove.com.au; Mon–Fri

10am–4pm, Sat–Sun by appointment; by car
Ferngrove's first vintage was produced in 2000, and it hasn't looked back. Known for estate-grown, cool climate wines, Ferngrove continues to win awards. In his 2011 *Australian Wine Companion*, esteemed Australian wine critic, James Halliday, awarded the winery five out of five stars for the seventh consecutive year.

Howard Park
Scotsdale Road, Denmark; tel: 08-9848 2345; www.howard parkwines.com.au; daily 10am–4pm; by car
Howard Park's wines are highly awarded and have been commended Australia-wide. Special tours of the winery are available if you arrange it in advance.

Margaret River

By far the most prestigious and well-known region is Margaret River. Renowned as a producer of robust Cabernets since the 1970s, it has since forged a reputation for crisp white wines, notably Chardonnay and Semillon

Below: the Australia flag flies proudly over the Voyager Estate.

Left: enjoying a day out in the Swan Valley.

Family-owned boutique winery noted for its Chardonnays. Those in the know love it.

Vasse Felix
Cnr Caves and Harmans roads, South Cowaramup; tel: 08-9756 5050; www.vassefelix.com.au; daily; by car

First commercial winery to be established in Margaret River; has an excellent display of modern art in the grounds, and an extensive Aboriginal art gallery. The restaurant is exceptional. They are known for their sparkling wines, and have small plantings of interesting grapes, such as Tempranillo.

Voyager Estate
Stevens Road, Margaret River; tel: 08-9757 6354; www.voyagerestate.com.au; daily; by car

Voyager Estate's entrance and grounds are as impressive as its wines. White-washed Cape York-style walls with rolling lawns, roses and beautiful buildings. You can't miss the gigantic Australian flag in the

---

Sauvignon Blanc blends. Its Shiraz has also won acclaim, and Merlot is widely used as a blend component. Home to estates such as Evans and Tate, Cullen, Voyager, Vasse Felix, Wise, Leeuwin and Pierro, and with more than 70 cellar doors, the region is a mecca for international wine-lovers. (Most wineries open daily 10am–4pm; see www.mrwines.com.)

For organised tours, contact **Margaret River Discovery Co.** (www.margaretriver discovery.com.au) or **Taste the South Winery Tours** (www. tastethesouth.com.au). If you prefer to visit the wineries independently, many of the best ones are on Caves Road and the roads leading off it between Yallingup and Gracetown. All are well signposted. You'll never get around to all of them, so pick a few that take your fancy and do them well.

Cullen
Caves Road, Cowaramup; tel: 08-9755 5277; www.cullen wines.com.au; daily; by car

Specialises in quality wines from single-vineyard sites.

Vanya Cullen's Diane Madeline Cabernet Merlot was recently classified in the Exceptional category of Langton's fourth classification of Australian wines. Cullen Restaurant offers one of the best vineyard views in the region.

Leeuwin Estate
Stevens Road, Margaret River; tel: 08-9759 0000; www.leewin estate.com.au; daily; by car

Family-operated winery famous for its Art Series Chardonnays, but it doesn't produce a bad wine. There is a large grassed area where each year the Leeuwin Concert is held – this black-tie affair is one of *the* events of the year.

Moss Wood
Metricup Road, Willyabrup; tel: 08-9755 6266; www.moss wood.com.au; by appointment; by car

One of WA's great wine estates, producing excellent Pinot Noir, Chardonnay, Cabernet Sauvignon and Semillion. Go if you can.

Pierro
Caves Road, Willyabrup; tel: 08-9755 6220; www.pierro.com.au; daily; by car

---

If you plan to visit any of these areas, you will need to drive, or be driven. There are some wine-tasting tours, but if you want to go at your own speed or off the beaten track, you are best off hiring a car and nominating a designated driver. Police do patrol these roads, and they conduct random breath-testing to determine if drivers are over the blood alcohol limit. Being over 0.05 blood alcohol means you will be fined, and possibly have your licence suspended. You also will not be allowed to drive any further, and if your passengers have also been drinking, you'll be forced to abandon your car. The best bet is just not to drink at all.

driveway. It is known for its whites, and the restaurant is good, too.

Wills Domain
Abbey Farm Road, Yallingup; tel: 08-9755 2327; www.wills domain.com.au; daily until 5pm; by car

Just off Caves Road, this relative newcomer produces some of the best Semillon in Australia – something different for the Margaret River region. The vineyard views from the restaurant are breathtaking; there's a gallery supporting local artists, large children's playground and grassy lawns.

Peel
Close to Perth is the Peel region, known for its Shiraz and Cabernet Sauvignon. It is not one of the bigger regions, but still produces good wines and is nice and close to Perth, making it handy for a day trip.

Peel Estate
290 Fletcher Road, Karnup; tel: 08-9524 1221; www.peel wine.com.au; daily 10am–5pm; by car

Established in 1973, this winery is one of the older ones in WA. The first vines planted were Shiraz, and then Chenin Blanc and Zinfandel in 1976, and others followed. The cellar door is a pretty, wisteria-covered place, and they encourage you to order ahead for picnics. Tasting platters are also available.

Pemberton and Manjimup
Pemberton region enjoyed rapid growth in the 1990s, and is noted mainly for its Chardonnay, with some Merlot and Cabernet Sauvignons also garnering acclaim. Its estates include Salitage, Mountford and Picardy. See: www.pembertonwine.com.au.

Manjimup is dominated by Chardonnay, Cabernet Sauvi-

Above: a golden vine in the Swan Valley.

gnon and Merlot plantings, and in the Blackwood Valley the main reds are Cabernet Sauvignon and Shiraz. Geographe is noted for the softer character of its Cabernets.

Picardy
Cnr Vasse and Eastbrook roads, Pemberton; tel: 08-9776 0036; www.picardy.com.au; by appointment; by car

The Pannell family are one of the region's stalwarts. Producing Chardonnay, Pinot Noir, Shiraz and Merlot/Cabernet varieties, all their fruit comes from their Pemberton property. They are very well respected and for good reason.

Salitage
Lot 3, Vasse Highway, Pemberton; tel: 08-9776 1195; www. salitage.com.au; daily; by car

John and Jenny Horgan are behind Salitage and are key players in the WA wine scene, having much to do with getting the Margaret River region going in the 1970s. Salitage uses only French oak barriques when barrel-ageing its wines. Try the Chardonnay. Salitage also has on-site accommodation and free winery tours at 11am.

Perth Hills
The Perth Hills area has been cultivating grapes since colonial days, but was only gazetted as a wine region in 1999. It now has 16 wineries

and 13 cellar doors, two of note being Darlington Estate and Millbrook. While both fall into the 'Perth Hills' wine region, they are a fair drive apart, Darlington Estate being east of the city, and Millbrook southeast. Both have excellent restaurants, for which you need to book.

Darlington Estate
Lot 39 Nelson Road, Darlington; tel: 08-9299 6268; www.darling tonestate.com.au; Wed 11.30am–5pm, Thur–Sat 11.30am–11.30pm, Sun 11.30am–5pm (restaurant only); by car

With gorgeous valley views as a backdrop, this is a great place to enjoy lunch or a romantic dinner. Free Wi-fi is available to guests.

Millbrook Winery
Old Chestnut Lane, Jarrahdale; tel: 08-9525 5796; www. millbrookwinery.com.au; light lunches: Mon–Tue, restaurant lunches: Wed–Sun; by car

Striking boutique winery in picturesque setting.

Swan Valley
Located roughly 30 minutes east of the CBD. You can pick up a food-and-wine trail map from the Swan Valley Visitor Centre in the historic Guildford courthouse (cnr Meadow and Swan streets, Guildford; 08-9379 9400; www.swanvalley.com.au; daily 9am–4pm). The trail takes in 32km (20 miles) of scenic

driving, as well as some 80 wineries, breweries and restaurants. Driving in the Swan Valley is easy, as there are really only two main roads. To get there from Perth, head out along Great Eastern Highway, taking the bypass, and then follow the signs until you get to Guildford. On Guildford's main road you will see a turn across railway tracks which is clearly signposted to the Swan Valley. As you make this turn, the Visitor Centre will be on your right; stop here for one of the trail maps.

The valley is renowned for its fortified wines, Verdelhos, Shiraz and Cabernet. Growing consumption at home and abroad led countless landowners to turn their land over to vines in the 1990s, and the resulting glut has made everyday wine-drinking extremely affordable. These bargains, known as 'cleanskins' because they are usually unlabelled, can only be found in bottle-shops. Don't expect such low prices at the vineyards, where you will find handmade wines of superior depth, style and quality.

The chance to try a wide range of wines and styles is enhanced in the Swan Valley by the diversity of vineyards, large and small, grand and humble.

Houghton
Dale Road, Middle Swan; tel: 08-9274 9540; www.houghton-wines.com.au; daily; by car
A valley stalwart, established in 1836, Houghton is WA's largest commercial winery. It has an extensive stable of wines, souvenirs and a restaurant, and holds concerts under the trees. Its most famous winemaker was Jack Mann *(see below)*. During his 51 vintages here he produced their White Burgundy, Australia's best-selling bottled wine.

Lancaster Wines
5228 West Swan Road; tel: 08-9250 6461; www.lancaster wines.com.au; daily; by car
With its unmade road and makeshift tasting shed, Lancaster looks humble, yet has some of the valley's oldest vines and most knowledgeable staff. It offers all the grape types that grow best here (Shiraz, Cabernet Sauvignon, Verdelho, Chenin Blanc and Chardonnay), plus a late-picked Chenin dessert wine. Good, strong local cheese is served, too.

Mann Wines
105 Memorial Avenue, Baskerville; tel: 08-9296 4348; Wed–Sun 10am–5pm; by car
Only those in the know get to Mann Winery. It's operated by Dorham Mann (son of Swan Valley vigneron Jack Mann),

Most cellar doors are open daily from 10am–5pm. Also, don't be put off by those that only open by appointment – people are very friendly, and only too keen to show you their wines. There is never any obligation to buy wine, either.

who only produces two styles of sparkling wine made in the traditional French Méthode Champenoise. They're truly something special and are available for sale from August until sold out (usually by December).

Sandalford
3210 West Swan Road; tel: 08-9374 9300; www.sandalford. com; daily; by car
One of the grand ones, although most of its excellent wine is sourced from its estate in the Margaret River area. This smaller property has won awards for its Cabernet Sauvignon and produces one, the Prendiville Reserve, that will reward anyone willing to cellar it for up to 25 years.

Sittella
100 Barrett Street, Herne Hill, 08-9296 2600;
www.sittella.com.au; Tue–Sun 11am–4pm for lunch; by car
A relative newcomer, Sittella is one of the most popular places to lunch while soaking in vineyard views with a glass of sparkling wine or its popular *petit verdot*.

Talijancich
26 Hyem Road; tel: 08-9296 4289; www.taliwine.com.au; Wed–Mon 10.30am–4.30pm; by car
Great fortified wines: tawny and vintage port, Muscat and Tokay. One of the only wineries in the country producing the Spanish variety, Graciano, and the first in WA to achieve Bio-Dynamic Certification.

Left: in the Millbrook winery.

Atlas

The following streetplan of Perth makes it easy to find the attractions listed in the A–Z section. The selective index to streets and sights will help you find other locations throughout the city

Map Legend

	Freeway		Bus station
	Main roads	✈	Airport
	Minor roads	❶	Tourist information
	Footpath	★	Sight of interest
	Pedestrian area	†	Cathedral / church
	Notable building	⚑	Statue / monument
	National Park	⬛	Tower
	Hotel	▲	Summit
	Urban area	⌇	Lighthouse
	Non urban area	⚑	Beach
† †	Cemetery	※	Viewpoint

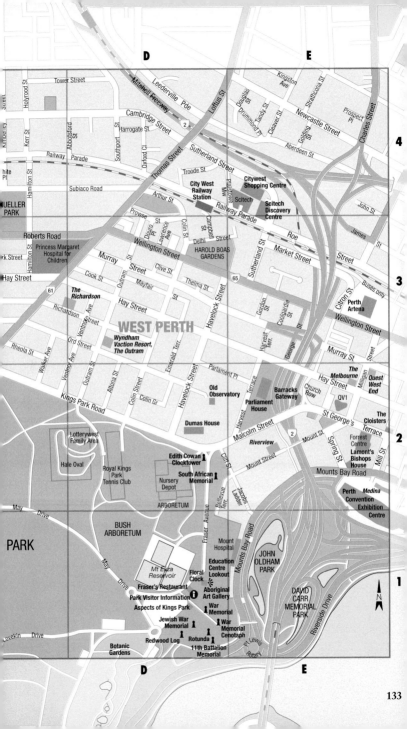

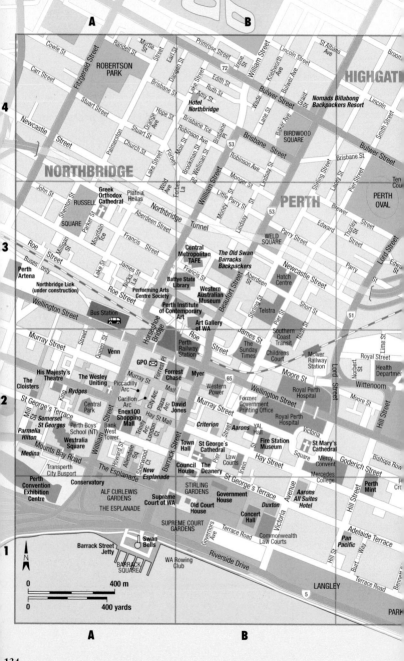

A B

Cowle St
Carr Street
Fitzgerald Street
Randell St
Myrtle Street
Earl St
Dangan St
Primrose Street
Irate St
William Street
Lincoln Street
St Albans Ave
Broom
HIGHGATE

ROBERTSON PARK
Stuart Street
Brisbane St
Edith St
Ruth St
Amy St
Wade St
Lane St
Bulwer Street
Knebworth Ave
Grant St
Bulwer Ave
Lincoln
Nomads Billabong Backpackers Resort

4
Newcastle Street
Hope St
Orange Ave
Church St
Stuart Street
Palmerston
Hotel Northbridge
Brisbane Tce
Robinson Ave
Wellman St
Muir St
Brisbane
Brookman St
Lane St
Baker St
Brisbane Street
BIRDWOOD SQUARE
53
Robinson Ave
William Street
Lindsay
Stirling Street
Brisbane St
Lacey St
Pier Street
Ten Cou
Bulwer Street

NORTHBRIDGE
John St
Shenton St
Milligan St
RUSSELL SQUARE
Greek Orthodox Cathedral
Parker St
Mountain Tce
Plateia Heilas
Aberdeen Street
Ward Ave
Forbes Rd
Northbridge
Monger St
Little Parry St
Morley
Lindsay St
PERTH
Parry Street
Edward
Brewer Street
Thorley Street
Lord Street
Edwa St
PERTH OVAL

3
Roe Street
Buses only
Perth Artena
Lake St
Nick's La
Francis Street
James St
Roe Street
Tunnel
WELD SQUARE
Central Metropolitan TAFE
Francis St
The Old Swan Barracks Backpackers
Aberdeen St
Newcastle Street
Hatch Centre
Short St
Parry St
51
Northbridge Link (under construction)
Wellington Street
Performing Arts Centre Society
Battye State Library
Western Australian Museum
Perth Institute of Contemporary Art
Beaufort Street
Stirling St
Telstra St
Short St
Southern Coast Transit
Lime St

Bus Station
Horseshoe Bridge
Art Gallery of WA
Roe Street
Perth Railway Station
James Street
The Sunday Times
Nash St
McIver Railway Station
Lord Street
Royal Street
Health Departmer

2
Murray Street
Venn
Queen St
GPO
Forrest St
Murray St
Forrest Chase
Myer
65
Childrens Court
Moore St
Norbert St
Royal Perth Hospital
Wittenoom
Moore St
Hill Street

His Majesty's Theatre
The Cloisters
Rydges
The Wesley Uniting
Piccadilly Arc
City Arc
Plaza Arc
Carillon Arc
Hay St Mall
David Jones
Western Power
Wellington Street
Former Government Printing Office
Royal Perth Hospital
Victoria
St Mary's Cathedral
Goderich Street
Bishops Row

St George's Terrace
Somerset
St Georges
Parmelia Hilton
Medina
Central Park
Perth Boys' School (NT)
Bank West Tower
Enex100 Shopping Mall
Trinity Arc
London Ct
Sherwood Ct
Allendale Sq
Barrack Street
Murray Street
Criterion
Town Hall
St George's Cathedral
Aarons
YAL
Fire Station Museum
Square
Mercy Convent
Mercedes College
Mount Bay Road
Westralia Square
The Esplanade
Howard St
New Esplanade
Council House
Law Courts
The Deanery
Irwin
St George's Terrace
Hay Street

Transperth City Busport
Conservatory
The Esplanade
ALF CURLEWIS GARDENS
THE ESPLANADE
STIRLING GARDENS
Supreme Court of WA
Old Court House
SUPREME COURT GARDENS
Government House
Concert Hall
St George's Terrace
Avenue
Victoria
Duxton
Aarons All Suites Hotel
Perth Mint
Adelaide Terrace
R Cro

Perth Convention Exhibition Centre

1
N
Barrack Street Jetty
Swan Bells
BARRACK SQUARE
WA Rowing Club
Governors Ave
Terrace Road
Commonwealth Law Courts
Riverside Drive
Pan Pacific
Hill St
Terrace Road
Bennett

0 — 400 m
0 — 400 yards
LANGLEY
5
PARK

A B

134

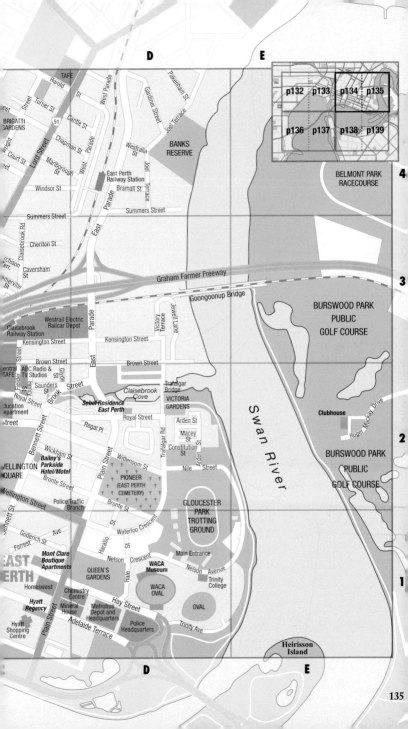

TAFE
Harold St
Turner St
Cantle St
BRIGATTI
GARDENS
Chapman St
West Parade
Gardiner Street
Pakenham St
Joel Terrace
BANKS
RESERVE
Lord Street
Marlborough St
Westralia St
West Parade
East Perth
Railway Station
Bramall St
Joel Terrace
BELMONT PARK
RACECOURSE
Windsor St

Summers Street
Summers Street

Claisebrook Rd
Cheriton St
Caversham St
East Parade

Graham Farmer Freeway
Goongoonup Bridge

Westrail Electric
Railcar Depot
Claisebrook
Railway Station
Kensington Street
Victory Terrace
Jewell Lane
Kensington Street
BURSWOOD PARK
PUBLIC
GOLF COURSE

Brown Street
Brown Street
East Parade

Central
TAFE
ABC Radio &
TV Studios
Saunders St
Fielder
Brook
Street
Royal Street
Education
Department
Street
Trafalgar
Bridge
Claisebrook
Cove
Sebel Residence
East Perth
Royal Street
VICTORIA
GARDENS
Clubhouse
Roger Mackay Drive

Bennett Street
Regal Pt
Arden St
Macey
St
Constitution
St
Swan River

Wickham St
Plain Street
Trafalgar Rd
Nile
Arden
Street
St
BURSWOOD PARK
PUBLIC
GOLF COURSE

WELLINGTON
SQUARE
Bailey's
Parkside
Hotel/Motel
Bronte Street
Wittenoom St
PIONEER
(EAST PERTH
CEMETERY)

Wellington Street
Police Traffic
Branch
Bronte St

Goderich St
Forrest
Haratio
Waterloo Crescent
GLOUCESTER
PARK
TROTTING
GROUND

EAST
PERTH
Mont Clare
Boutique
Apartments
Nelson
Crescent
Main Entrance
Nelson
Avenue

Homeswest
QUEEN'S
GARDENS
Chemistry
Centre
Hale
WACA
Museum
Trinity
College

Hyatt
Regency
Mineral
House
Metrobus
Depot and
Headquarters
WACA
OVAL
OVAL

Hyatt
Shopping
Centre
Plain Street
Adelaide Terrace
Hay Street
Police
Headquarters
Trinity Ave

Heirisson
Island

p132 p133 p134 p135
p136 p137 p138 p139

135

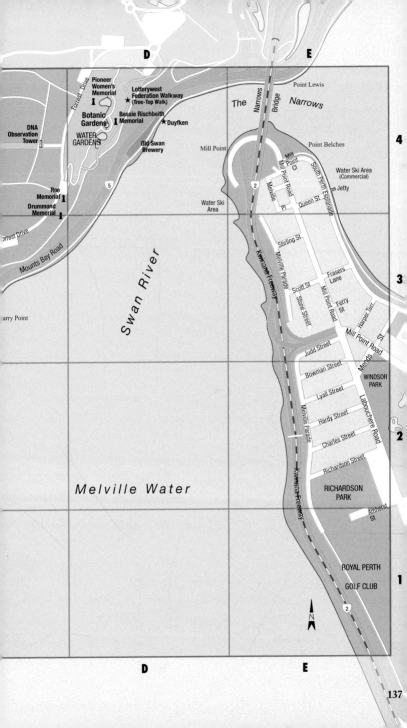

D   **E**

Point Lewis

Pioneer
Women's
Memorial

Lotterywest
Federation Walkway
(Tree-Top Walk)

The
Narrows
Bridge
Narrows

Forrest Drive

Botanic
Gardens

Bessie Rischbeith
Memorial

Duyfken

Point Belches

DNA
Observation
Tower

WATER
GARDENS

Old Swan
Brewery

Mill Point

Water Ski Area
(Commercial)

Mill
Point
Cl

4

South Perth Esplanade

Jetty

2

Melville
Pt

Roe
Memorial

5

Water Ski
Area

Mill Point Road

Queen St.

Drummond
Memorial

Stirling St.

Forrest Drive

Mounts Bay Road

Frasers
Lane

Swan River

Kwinana Freeway

Melville Parade

Scott St.

Stone Street

Mill Point Road

Ferry
St.

Harper Terr.

3

Mill Point Road

arry Point

St.

Judd Street

Mends

Bowman Street

WINDSOR
PARK

Lyall Street

Melville Parade

Hardy Street

Labouchere Road

2

Charles Street

Melville Water

Kwinana Freeway

Richardson Street

RICHARDSON
PARK

Amherst
St.

ROYAL PERTH

1

GOLF CLUB

N

2

D   **E**

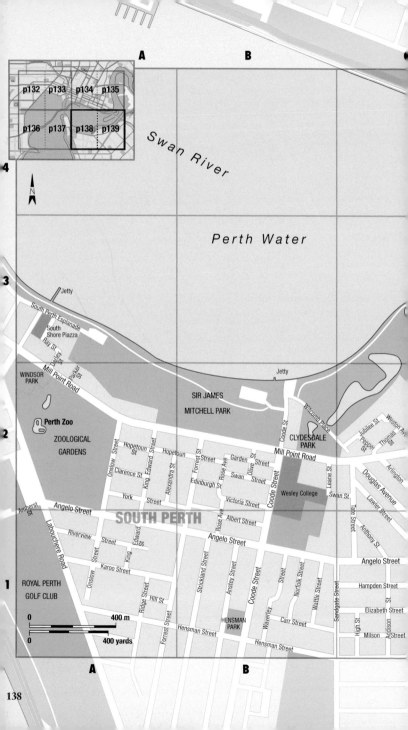

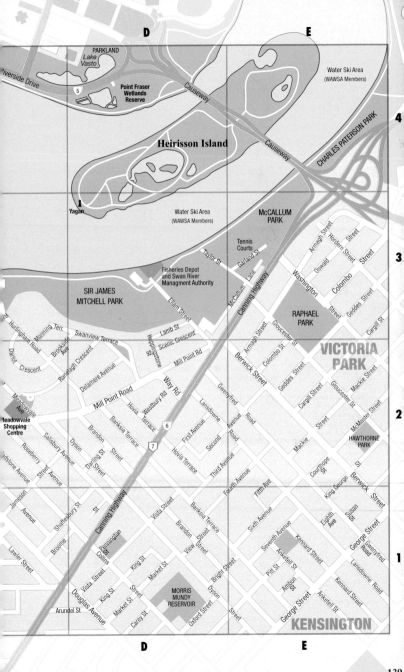

Riverside Drive

PARKLAND
Lake
Vasto

Point Fraser
Wetlands
Reserve

5

Causeway

Water Ski Area
(WAWSA Members)

Causeway

CHARLES PATERSON PARK

4

Heirisson Island

Yagan

Water Ski Area
(WAWSA Members)

McCALLUM
PARK

Tennis
Courts

Garland St

McCallum
Lane

Washington

Armagh Street

Hordern Street

Oswald

Colombo

Street

Geddes Street

Cargill St

3

Taylor St

Fisheries Depot
and Swan River
Managment Authority

Ellam Street

SIR JAMES
MITCHELL PARK

Canning Highway

Street

RAPHAEL
PARK

Colombo St

Geddes Street

Cargill Street

Hurlingham Road

Manning Terr.

Brookside Ave

Swanview Terrace

Lamb St

Happingstone
Scenic Crescent

Mill Point Rd

Armagh Street

Gloucester St

**VICTORIA
PARK**

Darlot Crescent

Ranelagh Crescent

Delamere Avenue

Way Rd

Berwick Street

Colombo St

Geddes Street

Cargill Street

Gloucester St.

Mackie Street

McMaster Street

2

Meadowvale
Avenue

Mill Point Road

Hovia Terrace

Westbury Rd

6

Lansdowne

Gwenyfred

Avenue Road

First Avenue

Second

Mackie

Street

HAWTHORNE
PARK

Meadowvale
Shopping
Centre

Salisbury Avenue

Brandon

Banksia Terrace

Darling Street

Dyson

Street

Hovia Terrace

Third Avenue

Courthope St.

King George Berwick Street

Roseberry
Gladstone Avenue

Avenue
Street

Jameson

Avenue

Shaftesbury St.

St

Canning Highway

Vista Street

Banksia Terrace

Brandon
Street

View Street

Fourth Avenue

Fifth Ave

Sixth Avenue

Kennard Street

Eighth
Ave

Susan

George Street

Gwenyfred
Road

Lansdowne Road

1

Broome

Pannington

Collins

King St

Seventh Avenue

Anketell St

Pitt St

Ambon
St

Kennard Street

Lawler Street

Vista Street

King St

Street

Market St.

Bright Street

**MORRIS
MUNDY
RESERVOIR**

Dyson

Oxford Street

Street

George Street

Anketell St

Douglas Avenue

Arundel St

Market St

Carey St

KENSINGTON

Selective Index for Street Atlas

Index

Insight Smart Guide: Perth
Compiled by: **Emma Green**
Updated by: **Jessica Zoiti**
Proofread and indexed by: **Neil Titman**
Copyedited by: **Pam Barrett**
Commissioning Editor: **Sarah Sweeney**
All photography by: **Glyn Genin/APA**
except: Art Gallery of Western Australia 76/77T; The Birdgeman Art Library 64L; Coo-ee Picture Library 64R; iStockphoto.com 2/3T, 8, 87C, 87B, 112/113; fotolia.com 65TR, 84; Paul Kane/Getty Images 5BR; La Trobe Picture Collection, State Library of Victoria 65R; Mecca Cosmetica 86/87T; Miramax/Dimension Films/The Kobal Collection/Penny Tweedie 56/57T; Newspix/News Ltd. 26/27T, 54B, 62/63T, 74C, 82, 112/113T; Newspix /Rex Features 56B; Pension of Perth 62/63B; Perth International Arts Festival 54/55T; Perth Theatre Company 116/117(all); Rise 84/85T; Rottnest Channel Swim Association 114/115T; West Australian Ballet 83B; Western Australia Tourist Commission 5BL, 5TR, 30, 50TL, 53BR, 54/55,

68, 70, 80B, 91, 122/123, 128, 129 130; Michael Willis/Alamy 40/41(all); Venn 97; www.photovation.com.au 36/37T
Cover picture by: **photolibrary.com**
Art Editor: **Richard Cooke**
Maps: **APA Cartography Department**
Series Editor: **Carine Tracanelli**

Second Edition 2012
©2012 Apa Publications (UK) Limited
Printed by CTPS-China
Worldwide distribution enquiries:
APA Publications GmbH & Co Verlag KG (Singapore branch); 7030 Ang Mo Kio Ave 5, 08-65 Northstar @ AMK, Singapore 569880; email: apasin@singnet.com.sg
Distributed in the UK and Ireland by:
Dorling Kindersley Ltd (a Penguin Company); 80 Strand, London, WC2R 0RL, UK; email: customerservice@uk.dk.com
Distributed in the United States by:
Ingram Publisher Services
One Ingram Blvd, PO Box 3006, La Vergne, TN 37086-1986; email: customer. service@ingrampublisherservices.com

Distributed in Australia by:
Universal Publishers; PO Box 307, St. Leonards, NSW 1590; email: sales@universalpublishers.com.au
Distributed in New Zealand by:
Brown Knows Publications; 11 Artesia Close, Shamrock Park, Auckland, New Zealand 2016; email: sales@brownknows.co.nz

Contacting the Editors
We would appreciate it if readers would alert us to errors or outdated information by writing to: Apa Publications, PO Box 7910, London SE1 1WE, UK; fax: (44 20) 7403 0290; email: insight@apaguide.co.uk
No part of this book may be reproduced, stored in a retrieval system or transmitted in any form or by any means (electronic, mechanical, photocopying, recording or otherwise), without prior written permission of Apa Publications. Brief text quotations with use of photographs are exempted for book review purposes only. Information has been obtained from sources believed to be reliable, but its accuracy and completeness, and the opinions based thereon, are not guaranteed.

London Borough of Barnet	30131 05057132 9	A & H	919.411047	
		Jan-2013	£7.99	

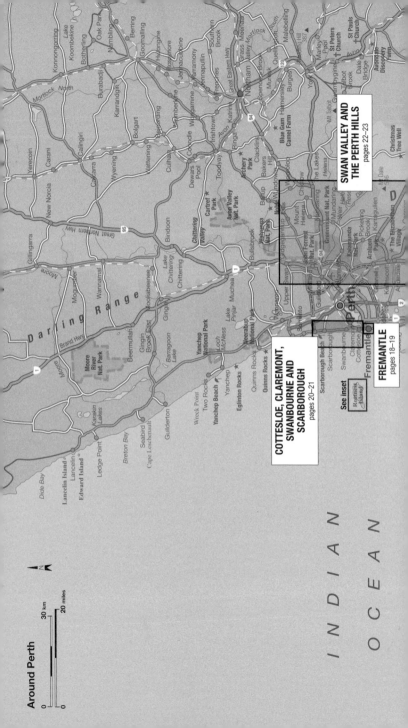